THE GREENHAVEN PRESS
Literary Companion
TO WORLD LITERATURE

READINGS ON

A DOLL'S HOUSE

Hayley R. Mitchell, *Book Editor*

David L. Bender, *Publisher*
Bruno Leone, *Executive Editor*
Bonnie Szumski, *Series Editor*

Greenhaven Press, Inc., San Diego, CA

Every effort has been made to trace the owners of copyrighted material. The articles in this volume may have been edited for content, length, and/or reading level. The titles have been changed to enhance the editorial purpose. Those interested in locating the original source will find the complete citation on the first page of each article.

Library of Congress Cataloging-in-Publication Data

Readings on A doll's house / Hayley R. Mitchell, book editor.
        p.   cm. — (The Greenhaven Press literary
    companion to world literature)
    Includes bibliographical references and index.
    ISBN 0-7377-0049-1 (lib. bdg. : alk. paper). —
ISBN 0-7377-0048-3 (pbk. : alk. paper)
    1. Ibsen, Henrik, 1828–1906. Dukkehjem.
2. Ibsen, Henrik, 1828–1906—Criticism and
interpretation. I. Mitchell, Hayley R., 1968–   .
II. Series.
PT8861.R43   1999
839.8'226—dc21   98-49695
                                                          CIP

Cover photo: Photofest

Copyright ©1999 by Greenhaven Press, Inc.
PO Box 289009
San Diego, CA 92198-9009
Printed in the U.S.A.

66Naturally, I shall not engage in any interpretation of my books: best that the public and the critics be left to puzzle over these as much as they wish—for the time being. I would simply and straightforwardly describe the circumstances and conditions under which I have written,—all, naturally, with the utmost discretion, leaving a wide area open for all sorts of guesswork. 99

—Henrik Ibsen

CONTENTS

Chapter 2: Nora

Chapter 3: Women in Ibsen

conditions in which women live—conditions, she says, that had not changed much since Ibsen wrote his play in 1879.

Chapter 4: Major Themes

FOREWORD

*"'Tis the good reader that
makes the good book."*

Ralph Waldo Emerson

The story's bare facts are simple: The captain, an old and scarred seafarer, walks with a peg leg made of whale ivory. He relentlessly drives his crew to hunt the world's oceans for the great white whale that crippled him. After a long search, the ship encounters the whale and a fierce battle ensues. Finally the captain drives his harpoon into the whale, but the harpoon line catches the captain about the neck and drags him to his death.

A simple story, a straightforward plot—yet, since the 1851 publication of Herman Melville's *Moby-Dick*, readers and critics have found many meanings in the struggle between Captain Ahab and the whale. To some, the novel is a cautionary tale that depicts how Ahab's obsession with revenge leads to his insanity and death. Others believe that the whale represents the unknowable secrets of the universe and that Ahab is a tragic hero who dares to challenge fate by attempting to discover this knowledge. Perhaps Melville intended Ahab as a criticism of Americans' tendency to become involved in well-intentioned but irrational causes. Or did Melville model Ahab after himself, letting his fictional character express his anger at what he perceived as a cruel and distant god?

Although literary critics disagree over the meaning of *Moby-Dick*, readers do not need to choose one particular interpretation in order to gain an understanding of Melville's novel. Instead, by examining various analyses, they can gain numerous insights into the issues that lie under the surface of the basic plot. Studying the writings of literary critics can also aid readers in making their own assessments of *Moby-Dick* and other literary works and in developing analytical thinking skills.

The Greenhaven Literary Companion Series was created with these goals in mind. Designed for young adults, this unique anthology series provides an engaging and comprehensive introduction to literary analysis and criticism. The essays included in the Literary Companion Series are chosen for their accessibility to a young adult audience and are expertly edited in consideration of both the reading and comprehension levels of this audience. In addition, each essay is introduced by a concise summation that presents the contributing writer's main themes and insights. Every anthology in the Literary Companion Series contains a varied selection of critical essays that cover a wide time span and express diverse views. Wherever possible, primary sources are represented through excerpts from authors' notebooks, letters, and journals and through contemporary criticism.

Each title in the Literary Companion Series pays careful consideration to the historical context of the particular author or literary work. In-depth biographies and detailed chronologies reveal important aspects of authors' lives and emphasize the historical events and social milieu that influenced their writings. To facilitate further research, every anthology includes primary and secondary source bibliographies of articles and/or books selected for their suitability for young adults. These engaging features make the Greenhaven Literary Companion series ideal for introducing students to literary analysis in the classroom or as a library resource for young adults researching the world's great authors and literature.

Exceptional in its focus on young adults, the Greenhaven Literary Companion Series strives to present literary criticism in a compelling and accessible format. Every title in the series is intended to spark readers' interest in leading American and world authors, to help them broaden their understanding of literature, and to encourage them to formulate their own analyses of the literary works that they read. It is the editors' hope that young adult readers will find these anthologies to be true companions in their study of literature.

INTRODUCTION: THE SCANDAL OF *A DOLL'S HOUSE*

Nora Helmer's last definitive act in *A Doll's House*, the moment when she leaves her family, slamming the door behind her, has been called by numerous critics the slam that reverberated around the world. It was a sound that echoed not only because Ibsen's plays were wildly successful at the time and the play was playing to audiences worldwide but also because of the controversies that slam awakened.

Suddenly, Ibsen's work was the topic of conversation—and heated debate—in newspapers, journals, on the streets, and in homes. As biographer Halvdan Koht writes,

> the legal question of whether Nora could actually be condemned for forgery by the letter of the law was discussed at length. Some questioned the plausibility of Nora's sudden rejection of that almost-inherited and well-drilled morality and her rebirth as a rebel. This was, in fact, the most meaningful question, but it was overshadowed by the problem that concerned the play's contemporaries most: was it morally right for Nora to abandon her husband and children for the sake of her own intellectual freedom? She was being judged as an actual person, not as a character in a play.[1]

The *Doll's House* controversy not only took place in the public forum, it also became an issue in some of the theaters themselves. One actress refused to play the last scene because *she* would never leave her children. And a theater in Germany even requested that Ibsen rewrite the ending altogether as it was too controversial for conservative German audiences. Ibsen acquiesced in order to maintain some control over the work. In this alternate version, Torvald leads Nora to the bedroom of her sleeping children. She crumples to the floor in their doorway, vowing to stay for their sake alone.

1. Halvdan Koht, *Life of Ibsen*, trans. Einar Haugen and A.E. Santaniello. New York: Benjamin Bloom, 1971, pp. 27–28.

Though it is interesting to read about, the *Doll's House* controversy is not the reason Ibsen's play has survived through time. It is the play itself that is universal and timeless; its ideas can still be discussed and interpreted today.

The essays in this volume reveal that the important struggle is Nora's search for herself—even though women's roles have changed dramatically since the play was written. This search for identity remains a motivating force for all individuals.

Contemporary critics also continue to explore other sociological questions of the play, such as the link between money and independence, the definitions of truth and freedom, and even the role of family secrets. Finally, *A Doll's House* is also discussed today for its technical faults and merits. Is that famous ending really too inconclusive for its own good? Who inspired the character of Nora? What did this realistic play contribute to the world of drama? These questions and others are raised in this collection and offer readers a varied and exciting introduction to criticism on Henrik Ibsen and *A Doll's House* in particular.

HENRIK IBSEN: A BIOGRAPHY

During his lifetime, Norwegian poet and playwright Henrik Ibsen wrote twenty-six plays and a collection of poems. He rose from being the son of a destitute merchant to one of Norway's most revered literary figures, contributing memorable plays to theaters worldwide. Ibsen's star did not rise quickly, however; he did not achieve his fame without struggle, and his work was not accepted without its share of political and social controversy. Ibsen persevered through theater closures that brought him great financial difficulty, and when his work was met with harsh criticism, he responded with more work. Eventually, his determination to succeed at his art won him both financial stability and critical acclaim, a goal that all writers strive for but few achieve in their lifetime.

Henrik Ibsen was born in Skien, Norway, on March 20, 1828, to Knud Ibsen, a merchant, and his wife, Marichen. His older brother, Johan, died shortly after Henrik's birth, thus making Ibsen the oldest of eventually four siblings who would join the family over the next seven years. In the early years, Knud Ibsen, who had inherited a substantial amount of money from his wife's father, was also successful in his own right, selling groceries, hardware, and other products from his shop and exporting brandy to Norwegian cities.

Skien itself was a bustling coastal town of two to three thousand inhabitants. It was active in industry and the lumber and merchant trades. Recalling his memories of living near the center of town, Ibsen writes:

> The air was filled the whole day long with the low, rumbling roar from the falls of Langefoss, of Klosterfossen, and many other rushing waters. Through the noise of the falls there was a sharp, snarling sound from morning to night, sometimes like the shrieks and sometimes like the moans of women. Hundreds of buzz saws were working in the falls.[1]

By 1833 Knud Ibsen was the sixteenth wealthiest man in Skien and invited to elite balls, dinners, and other engagements. Ibsen biographers are unable to pinpoint the exact cause of his downfall, but Knud's success was short lived. Beginning in December 1833 and continuing over the next two years, Knud's wealth rapidly declined. Many of his possessions, such as his distillery (also an inheritance from Marichen's father), livestock, and boathouses, were auctioned to pay bank debts and taxes. In June 1835, after selling off the rest of their possessions in Skien, the disgraced Knud moved the family to his summer farmhouse in Venstøp, located outside of town. Knud eventually fell from social graces, relations with his wife were estranged, and he was never successful in business again.

During this time, Henrik developed his reputation for being a lonely, brooding child. He shared many of his mother's interests, including painting, theater, and poetry. He was teased and even beaten by other children for his apparent bookish nature; however, Henrik did not take this abuse quietly. Annoyed by other children throwing snowballs and rocks against the house where he was reading or otherwise engrossed in his solitary pursuits, he "would tear after them like a demon and drive them off, then he would take out his anger by transforming them into monkeys or other animals in his caricatures."[2]

Ibsen's interest in the arts, and theater in particular, broadened during the heyday of traveling theater companies in Norway in the 1830s and 1840s. These traveling plays would mark the beginning of his theatrical education. As for his formal academic education, Ibsen walked from Venstøp to Skien for primary schooling, with hopes of someday entering into medicine. Beginning in 1841, he attended a local private middle school run by two theology students. His two years here gave him a broad education, including private tutorials in German and Latin, and introduced him to new literature. It was here that Ibsen first began to dream about becoming a writer.

In 1844 Ibsen's family moved back to Skien to live on a relative's property; Henrik, who had somewhat strained relations with his father, moved to the nearby town of Grimstad to work as an apothecary's apprentice. Life in Grimstad was no better for Ibsen. He lived in cramped quarters with his employer's family, the Reimanns. Much like Ibsen's father, Reimann, too, was heavily in debt. With the apothecary's dispensary housed in the same structure as the family dwelling, and customers needing assistance at all hours, for the first time in his life Ibsen found that he had no private place for himself, no quiet area in which to withdraw from others and read as he had as a child. His privacy was invaded, he had little free time, few friends, and he could not afford presentable clothes on his meager wages. Ibsen would later write, however, that he did not regret the six years he spent in Grimstad. He did, after all, gain some basic medical knowledge, his employer was good to him, and he was encouraged to pursue his hobby of landscape painting.

In 1846, when Ibsen was eighteen, he became romantically involved with twenty-eight-year-old Sophie Birkedalen, one of the Reimann housemaids. Sophie soon became pregnant and was sent back to her parents' house in disgrace. She gave birth to Hans Jacob Henriksen in October of the same year. Ibsen was ordered by the court to pay child support to Sophie until Hans turned fourteen. He obeyed this order, but he did not have contact with the child nor speak of the incident to anyone at the time or in the future. Biographer Robert Ferguson writes that it was as though "Sophie and her child never existed. The secret went inside him, intensifying his already secretive nature, developing into that obsession with guilt, shame, and Nemesis which is the chief characteristic of his art." [3]

In March 1847 Reimann's business, which was not doing well at the time, was auctioned to one of his previous apprentices, Lars Nielsen. Ibsen, who had acquired the title "Pharmacist's Assistant," moved in with Nielsen when he relocated the dispensary to a more central part of town. Ibsen's living conditions were much improved with this move as he had more personal space in which to live and study. He lived with Nielsen for the next three years, and he began to make friends among small groups of young intellectuals in town. Attracted by Ibsen's sense of humor and reputation for sarcasm, these intellectuals often met at the dispensary to be entertained by Ibsen's musings. Of that time Ibsen writes, "It was not in my power to express everything that was bubbling inside me except through foolish pranks and brawls, which brought on me the disapproval of all the respectable citizens who could not put themselves in the world in which I was struggling about on my own." [4]

Ibsen remained eager to entertain others, but what many did not know at this time was that he was also privately engaged in writing essays and more serious poetry than the lighthearted verse he often offered up to friends. His essays, for example, explored mature themes such as the importance of self-knowledge and the nation's preservation of the language and history of its forefathers. Ibsen's greatest achievement during this time, however, was the completion of his first play, *Catiline*, in 1849.

THE DRAMATIST'S FIRST EFFORTS

Catiline is a three-act drama in verse about the Roman rebel of the same name. Much of Ibsen's influence for this piece was the political revolutions in Europe during 1848, which stirred his own political development. "The young man cheered anything that looked like upheaval, a break with the past," biographer Halvdan Koht writes, "even though he had not yet formulated a [political] position for himself."[5] Hans Heiberg adds that, in *Catiline*, Ibsen "found a rebel after his own heart, comprehensible alike to the upper-class boy and to the apothecary's apprentice who had come down in the world."[6]

After its completion, Ibsen and his friends submitted the play to the Christiania Theatre under the pseudonym Brynjolf Bjarme, but it was rejected in December 1849. Ibsen's friend Ole Schulerud, who lived in Christiania (modern-day Oslo), opted to publish the play at his own expense in 1850; he printed 250 copies, of which 40 sold. Thus began Ibsen's career as a dramatist.

Ibsen accompanied Schulerud to Christiania in 1850 and took up residence in his attic-flat. He settled down to study in preparation for university matriculation, but he did not do well enough on his exams to enter the university and pursue his education in medicine. Instead, Ibsen turned to his writing, drawing encouragement from two positive reviews he received after the publication of *Catiline*, despite the fact that he had been forced to sell the remaining unbound copies of the play as wrapping paper on the street corner because he had no steady income. This belief in his work quickly paid off, however. By the summer of 1850, Ibsen's second play, *Warrior's Barrow*, was accepted by the Christiania Theatre and performed on September 26.

Ibsen's life took another dramatic turn late in 1851, when he teamed up with renowned violinist Ole Bull. Bull had opened his own theater in Bergen the year before, and he had plans to make it a great national theater, a place to showcase Norwegian plays by Norwegians. Eager to become involved in Bull's project, Ibsen contributed a song and poems to one of his musicals. His work was highly praised in the local papers after the performance, prompting Bull to hire Ibsen to assist the theater as a "dramatic author." It was the first time he was to receive a salary, twenty dollars a month, for his writing.

In addition to giving Ibsen this opportunity to assist with writing, the Bergen theater also offered him a grant to travel to Denmark and Germany to study stage direction and other practical theatrical matters. Upon his return, Ibsen promised to work as a stage manager and director in Bergen under a five-year contract. During his trip, which began in April 1852, Ibsen not only learned the intricacies of stage machinery and direction techniques, but he also made numerous contacts with other playwrights and worked to get them to write for the theater in Bergen. Running low on funds, Ibsen returned to Bergen in July 1852, assuming the role of stage manager, supervising scenes, dialogue, costumes, and set decor.

Fully entrenched now in his theater apprenticeship in Bergen, Ibsen next agreed to write one play a year for the theater beginning in 1853. His first effort was *St. John's Night*, of which Ibsen would later write, "The play is a wretched thing, not really from *my* hand. It is built on a poor, dilettantish draft sent to me by a fellow student, which I revised and put my name to, but which I cannot now possibly claim."[7] Not surprisingly, the play, which was full of brownies, elves, and folk imagery that was more Danish than Norwegian, failed at the theater. Audiences were not at all receptive to the work, and the play was only performed once.

For his next offering, Ibsen returned to *Warrior's Barrow;* reworking much of the verse and dialogue, he presented it to the theater in 1853. This play failed as well, however, playing for only three engagements. Ibsen encountered yet another failure with *Lady Inger* in 1855. A historical drama, the play's core theme was the struggle of Norway against Danish rule and the question of why Norway lost its independence in the Middle Ages. Although the play was criticized for factual inaccuracy—there was no Norwegian resistance to Danish rule in the Middle Ages—it did speak to Ibsen's era of intense nationalism. Ibsen also considered the play his best work to date, despite criticism and its brief run of two performances. "He knew he had done a good job," Koht writes, "His soul was in the work and the work revealed his soul. He was on firm ground now—his own."[8]

FINALLY, SUCCESS

Ibsen's first dramatic triumph came with his fifth full-length play, *The Feast at Solhaug*. The direct influence of this play was the great heritage of Icelandic sagas. "In the Icelandic sagas," Ibsen says, "I found in rich measure the flesh and blood embodiment of the moods and ideas that were taking shape, more or less clearly, in my mind."[9] The play was more lyrical than his previous work, much like the Norwegian ballads that he was also studying at the time. The audience was duly impressed by the poetry of the piece when it was first performed in 1856. Ibsen had finally received popular acclaim.

The Feast of Solhaug played for six more performances in Bergen, a lengthy run for so small a city. Its success, however, was not limited to Bergen alone. In the same year it was performed at the Christiania Theatre, and it was later translated into Swedish and performed in Stockholm and Copenhagen. While critical reviews were not always favorable, audiences continued to respond well to the play, and Ibsen would later look back and note this period as his happiest time in Bergen. Seemingly, Ibsen had now earned respect as a playwright, but this first success did not ensure similar fame for him in the near future. Indeed, his next play, *Olaf Liljekrans*, the last play he would write specifically for the Bergen theater, echoed the response of his earlier efforts: It failed miserably after only two performances.

MARRIAGE AND A NEW LIFE

It was also in 1856 that Ibsen met Suzannah Thoresen, the nineteen-year-old daughter of a priest who had chestnut-brown hair that fell to her feet. Ibsen was twenty-eight at the time. The two first met at a literary gathering at the Thoresen house and were introduced by Suzannah's stepmother, Magdalene, who was a patron of Norwegian theater in Bergen. They met again at a ball a few days later and, after spending the entire evening talking to each other, Ibsen found himself in love. He proposed within a month, and they married in 1858. Suzannah then "became everything to him," Robert Ferguson writes. "She was his helpmate, his comforter, his best friend, his reference book, and above all his muse."[10]

During their courtship, Suzannah and Ibsen were separated briefly by Ibsen's work. His contract with the Bergen theater was up in 1857, and even though he was able to renew the post for one year, he later asked to be released from Bergen in order to accept a position as artistic director at the Norwegian Theatre in Møllergaten.

The move proved to be a good one both professionally and financially, but as he was hired as a representative of the theater, he was under more pressure to direct and create plays that were more recognizably Norwegian. Whenever he failed in this task, his critics were eager to remind him of his post.

Ibsen's first project was the completion of *The Vikings at Helgeland.* When he finished the play he returned to Bergen in 1858 to marry Suzannah and bring her with him to Møllergaten. *Vikings* premiered there later that year in the Norwegian Theatre, but not without first encountering some controversy elsewhere. Feeling that the theater at Møllergaten did not have the right facilities for the play, Ibsen first sent it to Copenhagen, where it was rejected for being too crude. The Christiania Theatre later accepted it but failed to produce it. Finally, Ibsen decided to present it at the theater in Møllergaten. The play became Ibsen's greatest success yet, playing for eight performances and bringing in larger box offices receipts than his other plays.

Henrik and Suzannah's only child, Sigurd, who was named after a character in *The Vikings at Helgeland,* was born on December 23, 1859. After his birth, Suzannah announced that she would not consent to have more children. Both of them wanted to concentrate more on Ibsen's career. As Ferguson writes, "Both parties shared the religious notion of a call in their lives. . . . Suzannah's was to ensure that Ibsen became a great writer, and Ibsen's was the same."[11]

HARD TIMES

Despite the short success of *The Vikings at Helgeland* and lengthy runs of other playwrights' works that Ibsen directed at the Norwegian Theatre in Møllergaten, the theater was faced with increased competition from other theaters and rising rent and production costs. Ibsen's annual reports showed good ticket sales for the company, but the theater continued to run at a loss. In addition, the theater began to lose its audience.

At the time, the public taste for entertainment was leaning more toward the slapstick comedy and dancing girls featured in other theaters. And when the Norwegian Theatre did give in and produce what the public wanted, it was harshly criticized for neglecting its Norwegian traditions. In this climate, Ibsen began to lose interest in his duties at the theater, and by 1862 the company declared bankruptcy, placing much of the blame for its failure on Ibsen's general lack of commitment.

Ibsen lost his job after the bankruptcy and the Norwegian Theatre joined forces with its rival, the Christiania Theatre. Needing a break from drama, Ibsen focused much of his attention on his first love, poetry. Much of his poetic work of this period is very nationalistic in nature, such as his heroic ballad "Terje Vigen," which was highly praised in Norway. Ibsen's break from drama did not last for long, however. In 1862 and 1863, for example, he wrote *Love's Comedy* and *The Pretenders* respectively.

Before he finished his final draft of *Love's Comedy*, Ibsen was given the opportunity for a new life adventure. He was awarded a state grant to travel through the Norwegian interior to collect folktales. Ibsen left for his trip in late June and traveled through mid-July. Upon his return, he reported to the grant agency that he had collected seventy or more previously unpublished tales. Ibsen biographers, however, suspect that he could not have gathered as much work as he professes, since the areas he covered in his travels were well known to earlier tale collectors. Only four tales from Ibsen's trip were ever published. Koht notes, however, that Ibsen's trip had not been in vain:

> He had seen and heard much that would become the material of his writing. He garnered a wealth of fresh impressions of nature and folk life of his country, and they would come to life with deeper psychological implications when he had succeeded in freeing himself of the constrictions of the last three years.[12]

Having not produced a full-length book from his travels, Ibsen found himself deeply in debt, much like his father before him. Creditors had already taken him to court in previous years, and his part-time appointment as a literary consultant at the newly reorganized Christiania Theatre in January 1863 was not enough to stabilize his finances. He managed to keep creditors at bay, however, and worked in earnest on *The Pretenders*.

His work paid off and was able to keep him afloat a little longer. Ibsen sold *The Pretenders* for publication in October 1863, and it was produced by the Christiania Theatre the following January with Ibsen as director. The little money he received from the play did not last long, however, so Ibsen looked for other sources of revenue. After being turned down for an annual artist's grant from the government, Ibsen next applied for, and received, a travel grant. This time he would travel to Rome and Paris, and his family would later join him.

SUCCESS IN ITALY

When Ibsen first arrived in Italy in 1864, he remained idle through the summer, taking advantage of his rare opportunity for a vacation. In the fall Suzannah and Sigurd joined him in Rome, where Ibsen accepted the post of secretary of the Scandinavian Society which offered him free housing. He began work on *Brand*, a "great drama on vocation and responsibility," Heiberg writes, "of being wholly oneself, in contrast to everyday half-measures."[13] Ibsen completed the play in November 1865, and it was scheduled to be printed in Copenhagen by Christmas of that year. Because of some misunderstandings with the publisher, however, *Brand* was not published until the spring of 1866. All the while Ibsen remained in debt, struggling to support his family. His luck was soon to change.

When *Brand* was finally published in March 1866, it was an immediate success. By December it was in its fourth printing, an unusual literary success for the time. Koht discusses the play's popularity:

> In *Love's Comedy* truth to oneself and sincerity were examined in one sphere, marriage; in *Brand* every man in every condition of life is forced to meet the same decision. For years to come, this theme would be the basic one of his work; for two decades the same theme would be the criterion by which creative writing in Scandinavian countries would be judged.[14]

In addition to the wild success of *Brand*, Ibsen attained another kind of victory that spring. In April he wrote directly to the king of Norway and Sweden, Carl XV, to ask for a government-sponsored writer's salary. "It is not for a carefree livelihood that I am struggling here," Ibsen wrote, "but for the calling which I believe unwaveringly that God has laid on me—this calling to do what I believe Norway needs most urgently of all, to awaken the people and make them think."[15]

Ibsen's appeal for funding could not have been better planned. *Brand* was creating a sensation throughout Scandinavia. With the critics lavishing him with praise and the public rapidly buying out the first printing, it is no surprise that Parliament approved his application for a grant. They awarded him an annual sum of four hundred dollars, enough to pay for housing and food, which he would receive for the rest of his life.

Financially secure for the first time in his life, some subtle changes came over Ibsen as he relaxed into his role of supported writer. Outwardly, he changed the look of his beard and began dressing in the styles of the day, not the over-worn, tattered clothes to which he had grown accustomed. Even his letters, once sloppily written, took on the appearance of careful calligraphy; their tone changed, too, Heiberg notes. They were more friendly, with none of the anxieties of his earlier days.

During this time, Ibsen wrote his next play, *Peer Gynt*, which grew out of legends of the Norwegian folk hero of the same name but also drew greatly from Ibsen's life and studies. The play was published in November 1867. *Peer Gynt* received criticism in Denmark but good reviews in Norway. In Ferguson's opinion,

> *Peer Gynt* is Ibsen's greatest play, one of the greatest plays ever written. In its sheer range it far outstrips anything else he had written before or would write in the future. Never again was he able to play so fruitfully with the burden of consciousness, never again did he dare so openly to implicate himself in all his glorious, generous and instructive satires on human frailty and folly.[16]

A SELF-IMPOSED EXILE

When Ibsen left Norway for Italy, he considered his leaving an exile of sorts. He was bored in Norway, discontented with its politics, alienated from his parents, and he felt both physically and spiritually constricted. He even turned down a directorship at the Christiania Theatre, despite his poverty. "The thing is," Ibsen wrote even some twenty years later, "that I would be quite unable to write freely and frankly up there, which is to say that I would not be able to write at all."[17]

Ibsen also had feelings of bitterness toward his homeland. In 1867 he learned that creditors had seized his belongings in 1864, after he had departed for Italy. In addition to his furniture, paintings, and other items he had left in storage at the Norwegian Theatre, creditors had taken his letters and manuscripts and had sold them at auction. Ibsen was distressed that his private effects could be seized by strangers. Although Ibsen had talked of returning to Norway during his stay in Italy, he did not.

After the publication of *Peer Gynt*, Ibsen headed to Germany in 1868, where he would live in Dresden for the next six years. In Dresden, Ibsen wrote his next play, *The League of Youth*. Unlike his last two plays that were intended to be read, not performed, this new play, a political comedy, was written specifically for the theater. Ibsen also left the world of folklore behind and entered the realm of realism. *The League of Youth* premiered in December 1869.

HONORS AND TRAVELS

Between 1869 and 1871 Ibsen received the first of a number of honors in his life, and he was again rewarded with the opportunity to travel before completely settling down in Dresden. Ibsen received a grant from the Norwegian government to study art, literature, and culture in Sweden. He left for Stockholm in mid-July 1869. While in Stockholm he was well received and introduced to artists, writers, the social elite, and even royalty. Before his departure from Sweden in September, he was summoned to the royal palace by King Carl and made a knight of the Order of Vasa.

In addition to being knighted, Ibsen was appointed by King Carl as a Norwegian delegate for the dedication ceremonies of the Suez Canal. He left Marseilles, France, on a steamer bound for Egypt in October 1869 and was part of the first fleet of ships to travel through the canal in November. In Egypt, Ibsen received a fourth honor: being appointed commander third class of the Turkish Medjidjie order.

Upon returning to Dresden after his Egypt trip, Ibsen spent the year arranging his travel notes, catching up on correspondence, revising *The Pretenders,* and putting together a collection of poetry. He did not produce a new play during this period, but in January 1871 he was bestowed with another honor. This recognition came from Denmark, which declared him a knight of Dannebrog. This new honor renewed his confidence in his work and his position in society. "It is undeniable that Ibsen's social ascent during these years, along with his triumphs as a writer, freed him from the inferiority complex that had ridden him from his youth," Koht writes. "A decoration was an outward sign of this victory."[18]

Another victory for Ibsen was the publication of his selected poems in May 1871. To Ibsen, the book of fifty-five poems represented the various periods of development in his writing life. Ibsen's book, simply titled *Poems,* was as popular as his latest plays and went through five printings between 1871 and 1886.

EMPERORS, PILLARS, AND GLORY

Ibsen's first play after the release of his poems was the historical play *The Emperor and the Galilean,* about the Roman emperor Julian the Apostate, who had rebelled against the Christian Church. Ibsen thoroughly researched the historical background for the play and spent six months writing it. He planned to represent a more positive outlook on life, as his critics had called for something less pessimistic.

"The affirmative philosophy the critics have demanded from me, they can find here," Ibsen writes about the play, an affirmation that is made in *The Emperor and the Galilean's* view of the "third empire." Of this empire, Ibsen writes, "an age will soon dawn when the political and the social will cease to exist in their present form, but out of both concepts will grow mankind's happiness."[19] While one is not left with a clear conception of these ideas in the play, and friends of Ibsen even admitted at the time that they thought he was talking nonsense, the play did fuel philosophical discussion and various interpretations when it appeared in October 1873. In fact, the play sold out the first day of publication, and after reprints, over four thousand copies of the play were sold before the end of the year.

The publication of *The Emperor and the Galilean* marked a period of increasing glory for Ibsen. Over the next few years he received one honor after another for his work. In 1873, in connection with the coronation of King Oscar II, Ibsen received Norway's greatest honor, the Knight's Order of St. Olaf. The next year, student admirers met him with an honorary torchlight procession during a trip to Christiania. In addition to these accolades, various theaters were reviving productions of his earlier works, and critical analyses of his plays continuously appeared in English journals after first coming out in 1872. During this period many of Ibsen's plays were translated into other European languages, and *The Emperor and the Galilean* became the first of Ibsen's works to be fully translated into English. Finally, in 1877 he received an honorary doctorate from the University of Uppsala in Sweden.

Though things were going well for Ibsen personally, this was a period of political strain in Norway in which the Conservative Party was hostile toward the intellectual freedom of ideas. Ibsen had always resisted party politics but, as a writer, intellectual freedom—the freedom to create and think freely about religion and science and the human condition—was important to him. Ibsen had these ideas in mind when he wrote *Pillars of Society*, published in October 1877.

It was the first of what would come to be called his "social plays" and, following the example of his last two plays, it was immediately successful. In 1880 it also became the first of Ibsen's plays performed on the English stage. Ibsen wrote that the theme of this play is "liberation from all narrow conventions, a free and beautiful new life"[20]; truth and freedom, he believed, were the pillars of society, an ideal that he certainly repeated in later plays, especially *A Doll's House*.

A Doll's House

A Doll's House was the second of Ibsen's social plays. It was published in 1879 and premiered at the Royal Theatre in Copenhagen; by March 1880, it was still playing to sold-out crowds in theaters in Stockholm, Christiania, Bergen, Munich, Moscow, and elsewhere. *A Doll's House* was also the first of his plays to be performed in the United States. Renamed *The Child Wife*, the play opened in Milwaukee in 1882. In 1889 it also played in London and became the first of Ibsen's plays to run without adaptations in Britain.

Like *Pillars of Society*, *A Doll's House* addresses themes of truth and freedom, but it does so specifically within the frameworks of marriage and women in society. In his notes for the play, Ibsen's concern for women is clear: "A woman cannot be herself in contemporary society," he writes. "It is exclusively a male society, with laws written by men and with prosecutors and judges who judge women's behavior from the male standpoint."[21]

Ferguson writes that it was writing about women that allowed Ibsen to begin to understand the complexities of women. In *A Doll's House* he was able to explore these complexities in a contemporary and realistic setting. Although his biographers note that, compared to his contemporaries, Ibsen was slow in his support of women's rights, *A Doll's House* calls for the freedom of women nonetheless. True to his resistance to join any cause, however, Ibsen claimed that his purpose in writing the play was not necessarily to champion women's rights, but human rights.

Despite his claims, Ibsen's actions during the period he was writing *A Doll's House* suggest otherwise. For instance, he encouraged a Danish woman to begin a magazine catered specifically toward women, he asked that a woman be hired as the head librarian of the Scandinavian Society, and he agreed that women should have the right to vote.

Criticism and Mixed Reviews

After *A Doll's House*, Ibsen published ten more plays between the years of 1881 and 1899. The first of these plays, published in 1881, was the controversial *Ghosts*. Ferguson notes, for example, that the overt themes of the play included syphilis, free love, prostitution, heredity, survival of the fittest, and euthanasia. This time, however, the controversial nature of the play did not add to its success. Theaters refused to produce the work, calling it void of moral value; thus, *Ghosts* turned out to be as big a failure as Ibsen's early plays before *Brand.*

Ibsen was living in Rome in 1882 while his son completed his law school exams there. Before the end of the summer, Sigurd defended his doctoral thesis; at age twenty-two, he became one of the youngest persons in Rome to earn a Ph.D. It was during this time that Ibsen completed the first draft of his next play, *An Enemy of the People.* The plot of the play has been described as a simple tale of good and evil in which the hero's ideas reach well beyond that of the public majority. Critics were quick to point out the play's ambiguities, however; although the play was performed, it did not sell well in print form.

Ibsen's next play was *The Wild Duck* in 1884. It was another contemporary piece about the search for harmony between freedom and the old ideal of duty to country. Like *An Enemy of the People,* it was not well received, and critics found it difficult to understand. Ibsen encountered the same criticism with *Rosmersholm* in 1886. Ibsen describes this play as: "the struggle that every serious person has to engage in with himself in order to bring his life conduct into harmony with his understanding. . . . First and foremost the play is, of course, a literary work about human beings and human destinies."[22] In *Rosmersholm,* Ibsen had enjoyed exploring human psychology and creating characters from his imagination, but, unfortunately, this play was even less understood than *The Wild Duck.*

Likewise, Ibsen's next play, *The Lady from the Sea* (1888), received some initial interest, but it did not run for long on the stage. It was described as a mystical and romantic piece with the theme of balancing freedom with responsibility. In his notes for the play, Ibsen describes the heroine and her situation:

> She has come from the open sea, where her father's parsonage lay. Grown up out there—by the free open sea. Secretly betrothed to the irresponsible young coxswain—dismissed midshipman—resting throughout the winter because of damage to his ship in a foreign port. . . . The secret is in her marriage, what she hardly dares admit, hardly dares think of: The imagination's fascination with the past. With what is gone.[23]

The Lady from the Sea proved one of Ibsen's greatest successes in Christiania, but it received very mixed reviews elsewhere. Ferguson describes the critical response simply as one of "good-natured puzzlement."

THE PLAYWRIGHT LOOKS INWARD

Hedda Gabler, which was first published in 1890, also received a mixed reaction of boos, whistles, and cheers when it
premiered in Munich in 1891. The play marks the beginning
of Ibsen's return to more introspective work. It is also a return to the subject of the plight of women, as the talented
heroine, one of Ibsen's most memorable characters, is unable to carve out a niche for herself in the modern, male-
dominated world.

While the heroine is memorable, the play was puzzling.
Heiburg notes that it met with "almost total confusion all
over the world."[24] Fortunately for Ibsen, the mediocre reception of his latest string of plays did not prevent his work from
circulating. In the same year as *Hedda Gabler*'s premier, for
example, William Archer published the first collected edition
of Ibsen's work in English.

In 1891 Ibsen moved to Christiania without much explanation as to why he chose to return to his homeland after so
many years of exile. The first new play of this period was *The
Master Builder* in 1892. When it premiered onstage in January 1893, it did not receive a lot of attention, but before the
year was out, it was playing in various theaters in Scandinavia in addition to London and Chicago. Like *The Lady from
the Sea*, *The Master Builder* was a symbolic drama instead of
a realistic one. It is the first of a series of plays that explores
the effect of fame on the personality and the costs of success.

Admitting that the play contained more aspects of himself
than any other, Ibsen was now looking deeper within himself
for his material, rather than looking outside to the contemporary world. In the play, the builder suffers from the same
fear of heights that terrifies Ibsen. As Koht writes, "this fear
was a symbol of the terror that gripped him when he peered
down into the depth of his own soul, for in those depths he
saw the drama of a tragic conflict between the youthful
dream an old man clings to and the mounting doubts of his
own strength."[25]

Little Eyolf, published in 1894, also explores the theme of
success and self-delusion. The play centers around the
drowning of a crippled boy and the consequent exploration of
the relationship between the boy's parents and other family
members. Heiburg adds that it "concerns the man who,
meaning well, makes others believe in him, but who has neither the ability nor the character to fulfill their expectations,

and who is brought face to face with his own inadequacy."[26] *Little Eyolf* was a success. While the play was not well received in Berlin, it played thirty-six performances in Christiania and for four solid weeks in London to sell-out crowds.

Ibsen's next play developed the theme of success at all costs that he had explored in *The Master Builder*, and it also echoed the themes of money and independence found in *A Doll's House*. This play, *John Gabriel Borkman*, was published late in 1896. It was successful, following the same pattern of most of Ibsen's other plays of late. "The play came out in two first editions simultaneously, amounting to 15,000 copies," Heiburg writes, "and in the course of a few days it was published in a number of languages. In a few months it had been performed in theaters all over the world."[27] Koht adds:

> In Borkman he created a superman who believes he has the right to exploit everyone on behalf of the great things he wants to accomplish. In *John Gabriel Borkman* Ibsen lived through what might have been his own fate if his vision had not been great and his heart not full of love; there is a deeper tragic meaning in this play than in any other of his works.[28]

In March 1898 Ibsen was honored like no other Norwegian in history on his seventieth birthday. He received personal greetings from the king, and letters, telegrams, and gifts from around the world arrived for days. Various celebrations lasted for at least five weeks. Articles about Ibsen ran in newspapers throughout Europe, proclaiming him as the most influential dramatist of the age, and representatives from artist societies, women's organizations, theaters, and political parties gave speeches thanking him for his contributions to Norwegian literature.

Ibsen's busy schedule included attending numerous dinners and performances of his works in Christiania during the celebration. Special revivals of his plays also ran in theaters throughout Scandinavia and Europe, including Copenhagen, Stockholm, Berlin, Vienna, and England, and they were even celebrated in Japan.

Coinciding with Ibsen's birthday events was the publication of his collected works in German and Norwegian. The first installment was scheduled for release on his birthday. The release of the book was a huge honor for Ibsen, the finest birthday present. In the preface to the collection Ibsen suggested that his works be studied in chronological order: "Only by comprehending my entire production as an inter-

connected, continuous whole will one receive the precise effect intended by their individual parts."[29]

IBSEN'S LAST YEARS

The following year, 1899, marks the year of Ibsen's last contribution to the world of drama. This last play, *When We Dead
Awaken,* is often interpreted as Ibsen's final reckoning with
himself, and it was meant, Ibsen said, as an epilogue to his
three previous plays. It was published in a first edition of
twelve thousand copies, and the play was quickly interpreted
as an allegory of Ibsen's life. Some critics, in fact, believed
that the drama of the work was too private. The play was
widely performed and appreciated nonetheless.

When musing on themes for his final play, Ibsen won-
dered if his "writing had itself been life, or if he had sold his
life for his art and a poet's fame."[30] Professor Rubek, the ag-
ing sculptor in the play, exclaims, "When we dead awaken . . .
what do we really see? We see that we have never lived." Koht
suggests that "in the struggle between the demands of art and
the demands of life there is no solution but death. Only death
brings peace."[31]

Ibsen himself was heading into his final years after the publication of his last play. In March 1900 he suffered a small
stroke. Although he was not bedridden, the doctor advised that
he not work. Ibsen recuperated in a sanatorium and was much
improved by August of the same year. He was able to give some
interviews and go to short speaking engagements for a few
months, but in the summer of 1901 he suffered a second
stroke, which left him unable to write anything of length.

In 1903 a third stroke left Ibsen housebound and unable to
speak coherently. He wrote his last word this year: It was
thanks, scrawled on the calling card of Dr. Edvard Bull, the
physician who was treating him at the time. Ibsen's last years
at home were peaceful ones, spent in the company of family
and friends. Henrik Ibsen died in his sleep on May 23, 1906,
at age seventy-eight. He was given a state funeral on June 1
and buried in Our Savior's churchyard in Christiania.

While Ibsen's life work speaks for itself, Robert Ferguson
sums up his accomplishments:

> He created the modern theatre. He tried to show contempo-
> rary audiences that even without God it was still worth trying
> to live at a moral level, and in the pursuit of this vision lived
> out the truth of the professional writer's life: a lonely, hard,
> pot-bellied life, its pathos all but obscured by the blinding
> glare of fame.[32]

NOTES

1. Quoted in Halvdan Koht, *Life of Ibsen*, trans. Einar Haugen and A.E. Santaniello. New York: Benjamin Bloom, 1971, pp. 27–28.
2. Koht, *Life of Ibsen*, p. 30.
3. Robert Ferguson, *Henrik Ibsen: A New Biography*. London: Richard Cohen Books, 1996, pp. 16–17.
4. Quoted in Hans Heiberg, *Ibsen: A Portrait of the Artist*. Coral Gables, Florida: University of Miami Press, 1969, p. 36.
5. Koht, *Life of Ibsen*, p. 41.
6. Heiberg, *Ibsen*, p. 41.
7. Quoted in Koht, *Life of Ibsen*, pp. 79–80.
8. Koht, *Life of Ibsen*, p. 90.
9. Quoted in Koht, *Life of Ibsen*, p. 91.
10. Ferguson, *Henrik Ibsen*, pp. 64–55.
11. Ferguson, *Henrik Ibsen*, p. 70.
12. Koht, *Life of Ibsen*, p. 98.
13. Heiberg, *Ibsen*, p. 125.
14. Koht, *Life of Ibsen*, p. 208.
15. Quoted in Heiberg, *Ibsen*, p. 133.
16. Ferguson, *Henrik Ibsen*, p. 138.
17. Quoted in Koht, *Life of Ibsen*, p. 216.
18. Koht, *Life of Ibsen*, p. 262.
19. Quoted in Koht, *Life of Ibsen*, p. 286.
20. Quoted in Koht, *Life of Ibsen*, p. 302.
21. Quoted in Ferguson, *Henrik Ibsen*, p. 230.
22. Quoted in Koht, *Life of Ibsen*, p. 377.
23. Quoted in Heiberg, *Ibsen*, p. 248.
24. Heiberg, *Ibsen*, p. 257.
25. Koht, *Life of Ibsen*, p. 433.
26. Heiberg, *Ibsen*, p. 270.
27. Heiberg, *Ibsen*, p. 283.
28. Koht, *Life of Ibsen*, p. 443.
29. Quoted in Koht, *Life of Ibsen*, p. 449.
30. Quoted in Koht, *Life of Ibsen*, p. 456.
31. Koht, *Life of Ibsen*, p. 459.
32. Ferguson, *Henrik Ibsen*, p. 433.

CHAPTER 1

Evaluating the Play

READINGS ON
A DOLL'S HOUSE

A Doll's House Is a Myth for Our Time

Elaine Hoffman Baruch

Author Elaine Hoffman Baruch suggests that *A Doll's House* contains archetypal elements that account for the play's continued relevance. She discusses Ibsen's treatment of classical opposites, the theme of romantic love, and Nora's transformation, concluding that these elements contribute to the play's mythic proportions. Thus, the play carries a message not only for its own time but for ours as well: The good of the individual, and especially of women, needs to come before that of the social order.

"I ask you directly: is there one mother among thousands of mothers, one wife among thousands of wives, who could behave as Nora behaves, who would desert husband, children, and home merely in order to become 'a human being'? I answer with conviction: no and again no!" Thus was the world première of *A Doll House* on December 21, 1879, greeted by the critic and theatre-manager M.W. Brun. He was not an isolated male chauvinist. On the contrary, critical sympathy was almost entirely with Torvald Helmer rather than with his wife, Nora.

It would be a rash man today who would defend Torvald. If there is one work that qualifies as a myth of our time, it is *A Doll House*, if we mean by myth the embodiment of the ideals and aspirations of a sex. . . .

From a feminist point of view, Nora is the new adventurer, a mythic hero for women to emulate, a rehabilitated Eve who has the courage to leave the garden in search of knowledge. There is no aspect of the contemporary women's movement that Ibsen doesn't anticipate and comment on. In this sense, he may rightly be termed a seer. He questions all the underpinnings of our sexual politics: the assumptions of

Excerpted from Elaine Hoffman Baruch, "Ibsen's *Doll House:* A Myth for Our Time," *Yale Review*, Spring 1980. Copyright 1980 by Yale University. Reprinted by permission of Blackwell Publishers.

romantic love and marriage, the restrictions of the home in the nuclear family, the stereotypes of sexual polarization, the equation of functional with biological motherhood, the "nature" of femininity itself. He explores the nature of freedom for both sexes and considers the relationship of individual to past and future as well as to the family and the state. Finally, he questions the traditional view of history.

It is by raising the central questions about women in our time in imaginatively compelling forms that the play achieves mythical status. . . .

Viewed thus, a coherent reading of the play emerges in which all of the time-honored domestic truths are laid open to question and woman emerges in a new light. . . .

Insofar as the home is a prison for Ibsen, it is that for men as well as women. He gives the lie to the belief just born in the nineteenth century that home is a place where one can be oneself. On the contrary, the home is the training ground for our roles as actors. It is that for little boys as well as little girls, as Ibsen shows in his brief but pointed treatment of Nora's children.

The whole world of the Helmer household is a masquerade. Nora, the little doll, grows up to be a big doll. She wears a mask of "feminine" dependency, designed to please Helmer. This masking is literally revealed in the scene where she dances the tarantella in a costume brought back from Italy years before. The masquerade scene forms an ironic counterpoint to Nora's real part in the Helmers' Italian journey. Far from having been dependent, submissive, and entertaining in that episode, Nora had forged a signature in order to obtain money for her husband's travel cure. Much of her subsequent life with Torvald involves the attempt to hide this reality.

For much of the time she acts the part of a charming child, wheedling, cajoling, lying about not eating macaroons, and playing with her own children as if they were *her* dolls, thus insuring transmission of the problem to the next generation. But at the same time that she is acting, she is working—sewing, crocheting, embroidering, copying, all to pay back the debt she contracted to save her husband's life. Certainly much of the "problem" aspect of the play hinges on women's economic dependency and men's pride. Nora has to assuage Torvald's vulnerable ego by appearing economically as well as emotionally dependent.

IBSEN PLAYS WITH CLASSIC THEMES

One of the fascinations of *A Doll House* lies in Ibsen's treatment of classical oppositions: body/mind, feeling/reason, darkness/light, passivity/activity, gentleness/strength. The first member of the dualism has been traditionally associated with women, the second with men. We now refer to these dualisms as feminine and masculine stereotypes. Through his pervasive use of this binary mode of thinking, Ibsen places himself squarely in a mythical tradition. But by overturning the usual working of the mode, he becomes the creator of a new mythology. It is actually Helmer, authoritarian, rigid, correct, who is far weaker than the childlike, flirtatious, flighty Nora. It is he who turns out to be the creature of feeling, he who is a slave of the body, he who will be left in darkness at the end.

Torvald has never outgrown the need for things that Rilke, in an essay called "Puppen" ("Dolls") written some thirty-five years after the play, sees as the most obsessive preoccupation of childhood. The epithets Helmer uses—his wife is a lark, a squirrel, a sparrow—seem to indicate less her dependence than his, his reaching back to a childhood world of comforting pets and toys. At the moments that Nora angers him by her seeming stubbornness, she becomes that terrifying creature, "a woman," which is a term of abuse for Torvald, whatever it may have become in our own time. He cannot handle her then, for she no longer fits into the doll house. There is no question but that the doll house is more his than hers, for she is the one who leaves it while he remains.

Moderate feminists will blame the strains of the outside world for Torvald's need to create a doll house, in which everything—from mending to women—has to be attractive and in its place. . . . More radical feminists will see him as a villain and Nora as the victim of male arrogance and domination. Yet the play is more complicated than mere melodrama. At the end, when Nora speaks of becoming an individual like Torvald, she is still being in one respect duped by appearances. Torvald's freedom is as limited as hers. He too is a puppet. Though he is permitted to live in a doll house, which provides a kind of refuge from a world of increasing bureaucratization, in other respects he is never allowed to take off his mask of "masculinity," least of all by Nora, who leaves him when he does so. This is a point that many readers ignore, but one that indicates that men's freedom is tied up with that of women.

Nora is less fragile than her husband needs to believe, yet part of her "mask" has become real. She is not nearly as independent toward the end of the play as some actresses (or directors) represent her. What she longs for until the final moments is a romantic hero capable of being her savior; hardly a feminist ideal. And yet, as we shall see, this desire is perhaps not as far removed from feminism as might at first seem the case.

ROMANTIC LOVE

In *The Aesthetic Validity of Marriage*, a work Ibsen must have known indirectly if not directly, [Soren] Kierkegaard, in opposition to such cynical romantics as Byron, had argued for the existence of romantic love in marriage. If romantic love thrives on obstacles, then what could be more of an obstacle than marriage itself, the Dane asked with characteristic brilliance.

> When once there awakens an apprehension of love's proper dialectic, an apprehension of its pathological struggle, of its relation to the ethical, to the religious, verily one will not have need of hard-hearted fathers or ladies' bowers or enchanted princesses or ogres and monsters in order to give love plenty to do.

As if in mind of this passage, Ibsen has Helmer long to be a knight of marriage: "You know what, Nora—time and again I've wished you were in some terrible danger, just so I could stake my life and soul and everything, for your sake."

We expect no one to be a hero any more, partly because of such plays as Ibsen's. But within *A Doll House* the possibility of heroism still seems to exist. Immediately after Torvald speaks his aspiring lines, the chance comes for him to prove himself. But when he learns of Nora's forgery, this would-be knight fails the test, and attacks his wife in a loathing born of cowardice. His greatest fear is that of losing his honor or the appearance of it. For all his protestations of sacrificial love, his "honor" resides in the state, not his wife. It is his failure to live up to the chivalric ideal that causes the play's denouement, for, ironically, Nora's dream was the same his:

> TORVALD. Can you tell me what I did to lose your love?
> NORA. Yes, I can tell you. It was this evening when the miraculous thing didn't come—then I knew you weren't the man I'd imagined. . . . I was so utterly sure that you'd step forward, take the blame on yourself and say: I am the guilty one.

Kierkegaard had advocated a marriage of "candor, open-heartedness, revelation, understanding." These are our ideals in marriage today. But once the mystery and illusion disappear from the Helmer marriage, it is destroyed. In Kierkegaardian terms, Torvald never transcends the aesthetic. He is incapable of reaching the ethical. Nora too is unable to reach the ethical sphere, for as soon as Torvald fails to live up to her image of him, she rejects him. She leaves him, not, as her twentieth-century sisters might, because he shelters her too much, but rather because he does not shelter her enough. Once she sees that he is not a hero, she wants no part of him.

Ibsen here seems to deal a death blow to the myth of romantic love in marriage, at least that love which is based on illusion. At the same time he suggests a reason for the growth of Nora's self-awareness. What is more important for the play's status as myth, he suggests a reason for the change in many women's consciousness today. It is disillusionment over Torvald that provides the soil out of which Nora's feminism grows. In large measure the feminist movement is a revolt against the myth of romantic love. Feminists attack it as a tool of oppression, a propaganda device designed to keep women in the home. But theirs may also be a *cri de coeur* (cry of the heart) for something that has gone sour or something that is found not to exist. Many an individual feminist's history is not very different from Nora's.

Nora leaves to find herself. That's one reason. She also leaves to allow Torvald time to find himself. She doesn't give up her dream of a miracle, but now the "greatest miracle" would consist of their transforming themselves so that their living together would be a true marriage. If Ibsen had stopped here, a feminist interpretation of the play would hardly be possible, for it would seem to view marriage as the final solution to the woman problem, something that feminists refuse to accept. But Ibsen did not stop here. The possibility of divorce looms large when Nora slams the door. Thus *A Doll House* becomes a landmark play in the history of Western literature. It is not only a play about falling out of love, as Maurice Valency says, it is also a play in which divorce is posited as a potentially happy ending, at least for one of the members in a relationship. This is another reason for according the play mythical status in our time. . . .

NORA BECOMES A NEW EVE

Critics as temperate and astute as Elizabeth Hardwick and John Weightman ask why Nora didn't take her children with her. Even some feminists—those who advocate the right to single motherhood—condemn Ibsen for making Nora seem heartless and cruel to her children. Actually, it is less a desire for freedom than a great sense of inferiority and the desire to find out more about the male world outside the home that drives Nora away from her children. . . . Nora loses her faith in her moral right and ability to bring up her children when she finds out that the act she committed out of love is labeled a crime by the world at large.

One should remember also that, unlike our contemporary situation, for which women are not always thankful, custody in Ibsen's time was normally retained by the father.

Furthermore, Nora was not expected to have sole responsibility for the rearing of her children. That responsibility was partly with Anne Marie, the governess, who had brought up Nora herself. While Ibsen's contemporaries no doubt recognized this fact more than our servantless age is likely to, they nonetheless granted Nora a greater importance as mother than she felt herself to have. . . .

But Ibsen did not believe in making women feel important as mothers as a way of keeping them at home for the husbands. He rejects this time-honored means of control at the end of *A Doll House,* at least in the version that he chose to hand down to posterity. He did, however, write an alternate ending for the promoters of *kirche, küche,* and *kinder.* Ibsen said he was outraged at having to tack on a conciliatory ending for the German production, but because he was not protected by copyright laws in Germany, and knowing that his work could be tampered with by others, he decided to meet the German request for revision. In the alternative German ending, Helmer forces Nora to the door of the children's bedroom and tells her that, if she leaves, they will be motherless, as she was before them. This convinces her to stay. In point of psychological fact, Ibsen is more accurate in having her leave them. She is simply repeating a pattern made familiar in her childhood.

In another German version, not by Ibsen, after some time lapse Nora asks Helmer if she is forgiven. For an answer, he pops a forbidden macaroon into her mouth. Such an ending reduces Nora to a cartoon character of the old mythology. It reinforces her in the passive, dependent, submissive, coy role that is overthrown in the authentic version of the play.

For much of the play, Nora exhibits all of the "feminine" traits that Freud was later to find destined by anatomy: childishness, narcissism, passivity, maternality, irrationality, and lack of a sense of justice. Yet within the space of a few minutes she sheds them all. I do not think it was because Ibsen was interested in novelty for novelty's sake, or in giving dramatic shocks to his audience, that this happens, though these were the reasons suggested by his earliest critics. Rather, Ibsen is exploring the question of biology versus social conditioning and its part in social history, an issue that is very much in the forefront of thinking about women today. In her rejection of the doll house, Nora blames her environment, not her genes, for her her doll-like qualities. Considering her transformation, Ibsen seems to be supporting her feminist point of view. Her transformation becomes doubly credible when we realize that her so-called femininity was for much of her life largely an act.

Nora's awakening is typical and therefore archetypal; however, her characterization grew out of the stuff of reality, not myth. It was Laura Petersen Kieler, a writer, who provided the model. One might question why Ibsen changed the original model and deprived Nora of any special talents, but by doing so, he reduced the problem of feminine selfhood to that of kinship relationships, where in fact the greater dramatic challenge lay. . . . The public might have been willing to grant that a writer needs a room of her own; even today it feels otherwise about a mere wife and mother. Ibsen tried to show that every person needs a room that is larger than a playpen. . . .

Ibsen invests his heroine with a romantic emphasis on self that had been restricted to males earlier in the century. In a sense, the existential variety of feminism, which seeks personal fulfillment, may be seen as the last vestige of the romantic movement, for it posits the good of the individual over that of the social order. . . . It is Nora in this play who makes the choices; she is a revolutionary in that she seeks to break out of ordained categories for women. What is almost unique about Ibsen's treatment is that she does not do so through the usual route of sexual transgression with a man, the way of a Madame Bovary, for example. Instead, she acts by herself, without a man to aid her. . . .

Ibsen creates a new Eve; *A Doll House* offers a new interpretation of Genesis. Though Nora has done a forbidden thing in entering into a pact with that devil Krogstad, from whom she obtained the loan, her desire will not be to her husband nor will she be ruled by him (Genesis 3:16). She will go forth to seek knowledge, not through the intermediary of a husband, or indeed of any man, but rather by herself. Through her, Ibsen rejects what had been most prominent in the Western tradition, the vicarious existence of women.

A Doll's House Is Theatre of the Grotesque

Nancy Kindelan

Author Nancy Kindelan of Dartmouth College defines *A Doll's House* as Theatre of the Grotesque, similar to early twentieth-century Russian theater. Kindelan argues that Ibsen presents Nora as an archetypal character, who represents the human condition. Members of the audience first identify with the child-archetype in Nora, forming their own associations based on her, until they are forced to grow with Nora as she goes through the process of individuation. This growth is skillfully presented through Ibsen's use and exacting controls of symbols in the play that allow for a more "refined representation of reality."

As a late nineteenth-century playwright who has more often than not been associated with naturalism and realism, Ibsen (1828–1906) seems an unlikely candidate for the Theatre of the Grotesque. This form of theatre directly relates to the experimental studio work in Russia at the beginning of the twentieth century. . . . Yet, it has been recorded that [its adherents'] synthetic theatrical principles were being applied to Ibsen's plays: *A Doll House* (1879), *Rosmersholm* (1886), and *Hedda Gabler* (1890). A close evaluation of the Theatre of the Grotesque reveals an emphasis on the physical symbol as a way of unlocking unconscious thoughts and perceptions. In theatre, the physical symbol can range from the actual script requirements, to forceful scenic diction, to possibilities of character treatment. Each of these elements reinforces the other until the gesture (the physical symbol) unlocks subconscious thought and provides meaning which in its outlined

Excerpted from Nancy Kindelan, "Ibsen's *A Doll's House* and the Theatre of the Grotesque," in *All the World: Drama Past and Present*, edited by Karelisa V. Hartigan, vol. 2. Copyright 1982 by University Press of America, Inc. Reprinted with permission of University Press of America. Endnotes in the original have been omitted in this reprint.

form becomes a condensed, pure, and, in some instances, an archetypal statement. In this sense, the Jungian [Swiss psychologist, Carl Gustav Jung] construct of archetypes and the Theatre of the Grotesque are similar in both substance and form. It is the purpose of this study to identify their similarities by utilizing the Jungian "child-archetype" in an analysis of *A Doll House* thereby illustrating its relation to the Theatre of the Grotesque.

Evident throughout Ibsen's canon is the recurring theme of an individual's struggle against the forces of society, as well as an individual's struggle "for liberation from the forces of his own character which hold him captive." Whether the play's dramatic structure is poetic, realistic, or has expressionistic qualities, the idea of the individual's struggle remains apparent. Within Ibsen's dramatic vision there are larger implications which have been interpreted previously in mythic proportions. Traditionally, the myth is a means by which man can begin to understand some of the complexities inherent in the universe, as well as his history and possible destiny. . . .

Nora Is an Archetypal Character

Nora in Ibsen's *A Doll House* is illustrative of his ability to combine the historical sense with that of personal individual development to create a character that has reached mythic proportions. It is no longer necessary to identify this character as the Nora Helmer in Ibsen's *A Doll House*—the poor housewife who struggles against the insurmountable malevolent forces of a Victorian society. We can simply say "Nora" and the identification is complete. If there remains some doubt to the accessibility of this literary character to the knowledge of mankind in general, all that is necessary to prove the point is watching an audience identify with the character after a few moments of Act One. To a modern twentieth-century consciousness, Nora's self, her relationship, and her eventual development strike a familiar chord. Jung has identified man's ability to make these connections through the process of "the collective unconscious." The singular "collective" quality of Nora that makes this modern-day myth so potent is not the story so much as it is the character. Although the character of Nora has attained mythic proportions in a modern world that is concerned with women and their place in society, closer scrutiny will reveal that it is the archetypal structuring of this character that provides the link to the collective unconscious, establishes its universality, and allows a twentieth-century interpretation to be applied to a classical framework. . . .

Like myths and dreams, archetypes can be a means by which man can identify, organize, and understand the complexities of the human conditions. The archetype is, in this case, a human symbol—a connotative means of identification. To a member of the audience Nora and her distinctive childlike qualities and actions are identifiable not by logical facts that construct a didactic message. Instead they are recognizable by associations, automatic thought processes that occur in the psyche and form the collective unconscious, for in Jungian terms: "Contents of an archetypal character are manifestations of processes in the collective unconscious.". . .

"Archetypes are not mere names, or even philosophical concepts. They are pieces of life itself—images that are integrally connected to the living individual by the bridge of emotions." A motif that seems to be the archetypal content in Nora's character is that of the child. In Jungian psychology, "The child-motif represents the preconscious, childhood aspect of the collective psyche." Also, the "child-motif" represents the process of individuation, potential future, and evolution toward independence. The connection between the Jungian archetype of the "child-motif" and that of Nora Helmer is as obvious as it is multidimensional.

In the play's text, Nora is called specifically a "child" by Torvald and Mrs. Linde, and later she uses the word to describe herself. She acts like a child with her children, and she has childlike responses in adult conversations; although the observations become more difficult to identify specifically, they remain evident in her inability to reason and function in an adult fashion. The archetypal structure within the "child-motif" becomes more complicated as the dramatic conflict intensifies and Nora begins to identify her actions as being childlike, thus realizing her dependence, her insignificance, and her immaturity. The third act of *A Doll House* becomes, in Jungian terms, the process of individuation. In actuality, the child-archetype is met in the process of individuation. . . .

INSIDE NORA'S HOUSE OF SYMBOLS

Determining the dramatic symbols in *A Doll House* is useful not only in the development of a traditional, realistic interpretation, or as an essential component of a Jungian analysis, but is also fundamental to the theoretical understanding of, and the practical adaptation to, the Theatre of the Grotesque. In order to determine how the realistic symbol can be adapted to a more theatrical vision of reality, it is important to signify how the symbol is employed traditionally, as Ibsen carefully selects both linguistic and physical symbols to hasten and enhance the disintegration and development of Nora.

According to Jung's psychology, true liberation can only come from within: before a person or a character can become an individual he must realize his limitations, understand what kind of person he or she is, and strive to become that person. Ibsen attempts to apply this methodology in the evolution of Nora's character from that of a doll, or childlike character to a human being (individual). Corresponding with the development of the plot is the logical transformation of its central character. In the opening dialogue of *A Doll House*, Nora's character is equated to that of various animals, thus revealing a shallow relationship between husband and wife. The dialogue reveals that Nora is not a person in Torvald's eyes, but a plaything, a "little squirrel," a "lark"—a creation of Torvald's mind that satisfies the requirements of a nineteenth-century society which demands china-doll wives, not individuals.

The evolution of the individual is revealed not only through a collection of linguistic symbols, but also by the physical symbols: the Christmas tree, the Tarantella, the costume for the fancy dress ball, the wedding ring, and the application of light and shadow. These symbols demonstrate further the individual's struggle in her environs, her psychological conflict, and her emotional struggle.

The Christmas tree symbolically illustrates the happy, secure Helmer household. When that position is threatened by Krogstad's accusation, Nora does not regain her composure through logical reasoning; instead, she returns to the tangible symbol of the Christmas tree—which, to her, signifies security, warmth, the "happy" Helmer household. She tries to regain her composure by decorating the tree; in an empty house, she speaks out loud: "A candle here—a flower here—. The horrible man! It's all nonsense—there's nothing wrong. The tree shall be splendid! I will do everything I can think of to please you, dance for you—." Later, in Act Two, Ibsen's

WHEN ONE DOOR SLAMS, ANOTHER ONE OPENS

Nora's final slamming of her dollhouse door, symbolic of her emotional growth and new independence, is an act that has been analyzed and debated by numerous literary critics. In The Modern Stage and Other Worlds, *Austin E. Quigley illustrates that the door is not only a key image at the end of the play, however; doors are relevant symbols throughout the work.*

It should not be overlooked that the stage directions for the opening action focus prolonged attention on the very doorway through which Nora will finally exit in disappointment, disillusionment and anger:

> *The front door-bell rings in the hall; a moment later, there is the sound of the front door being opened. Nora comes into the room, happily humming to herself. She is dressed in her outdoor things, and is carrying lots of parcels which she then puts down on the table, right. She leaves the door into the hall standing open; a Porter can be seen outside holding a Christmas tree and a basket; he hands them to the Maid who has opened the door for them.*

This extended attention to the doorway at the beginning of the play should not be forgotten when we find ourselves staring at it once more at the end, and neither should we forget the momentary tableau of the unadorned Christmas tree framed by the doorway. In case we should be inclined to forget, the play draws attention to that doorway and others repeatedly throughout the action. The moment Nora is alone at the beginning of the play, she steals over to her husband's study door and listens to hear whether he is home. When Krogstad comes to call on her, Nora goes across and bolts her husband's door. When disaster confronts her, and Nora sadly notes that she has only thirty-one hours to live, she is interrupted by her husband, standing *'in the doorway'*, asking what has become of his little lark, and she moves towards him and the doorway *'with open arms'*. When Krogstad leaves after his concluding conversation with Mrs Linde, *'the door out into the hall remains standing open'*; our attention is focused on it and on the music wafting down from Nora's dancing upstairs. As we watch and listen, the outer door is unlocked, and Torvald *'pushes Nora almost forcibly into the hall'*, and, dressed in her Italian costume, she lingers reluctantly *'in the doorway'*. Torvald subsequently locks the front door to keep Nora in when her forgery is revealed. Furthermore, the letter which is to betray Nora's secret is conspicuously inserted into and obtrusively remains in the mailbox attached to the same outside door. Conversations or actions are interrupted repeatedly by the doorbell ringing, or someone knocking, and, in a play with several characters and a single set, exits and entrances are legion.

placement and treatment of the tree symbolically reflects Nora's subconscious: her false sense of security is gone, as well as her gaiety and the spirit of her fight.

The employment of heredity and environment (central components in the development of naturalism and realism) link nineteenth-century morality to the psychology of Nora's character. Convinced she is a carrier of a vile, corrupt trait inherited from her father, and possibly transmitted to her children, Nora perceives herself as vile, sinister, and immoral. The Tarantella, as a ritual dance, can be interpreted as Nora's attempt to dispel the evil she feels she has inherited and subsequently infected her home. Like the victim of the venom of a poisonous spider who can only eject the toxin from his veins through a wild, dancelike exhibition, Nora's actions are a final—but futile—attempt to destroy the poison symbolically, since she is incapable of eliminating her problems mentally.

The wedding ring, the symbol of the bond of marriage, is probably the most overt emblem. In the final moments of Act Three, and in the process of Nora's individuation, Nora returns her ring (the symbolic conclusion to their marriage, their lies, and her psychological ties) to Torvald. . . .

CONTROL OF SYMBOLS

Locating the physical symbols can give validity to a realistic interpretation of this play, but it can run the risk of leaving this drama without its due dynamic temperament. The multidimensional use of both the physical and linguistic symbols, and the archetypal structuring of Nora's character create a potential sense of theatre that is worthy of more than the techniques of late nineteenth-century naturalism and realism. Observing the theatre practices of this era, Anton Chekhov cries out, "Real. The theatre is art." Concurrently, the significance of Ibsen's plays does not lie in his ability to successfully translate [French dramatist, Augustin Eugene] Scribe's well-made play techniques, or to manipulate dramatic symbols until they convey the components of naturalism and realism. Instead, his contribution is in his attempt to provide magnitude to the ideological forces behind the play until their scope excites the senses on the most primitive level. Determining the magnitude of Ibsen's vision enables the theatrical practitioner to understand: "the didactics of Ibsen's plays are never from one character, they are inferred from a whole structure of character and action.". . .

Influenced by the twentieth-century artistic movements (symbolism, cubism, surrealism, and impressionism), the Russian theatre practitioners of the late nineteenth and early twentieth centuries were interested in the impact of the symbol as a means of unlocking an artistic vision that was a more refined representation of reality. . . . A careful manipulation of each symbol until it artistically synthesized the aesthetic idea became the fundamental force behind the Theatre of the Grotesque. [Theatrical producer Vsevolod] Meyerhold defines "grotesque" as a reconstruction of reality that has the potential of leading the audience to another level of consciousness. In Meyerhold's sense of reality, "grotesque" was a fundamental trait of the theatre:

> [The grotesque is] a deliberate exaggeration and reconstruction (distortion) of nature and the unification of objects that are not united by either nature or customs of our daily life. The theatre, being a combination of natural, temporal, spatial, and phenomena, is itself outside of nature. It finds that these phenomena invariably contradict our everyday experience and that the theatre itself is essentially an example of the grotesque.

According to Meyerhold, the production's central thematic idea, "the *jeu*," must be captured and appear in every aspect of the *mise-en-scene.* The style, "grotesque," is capable of penetrating the consciousness of the spectator by detailing succinctly the major idea of the production. By carefully identifying, organizing, and manipulating each symbol, the essence of the thematic idea ("the *jeu*") emerges as an artistic, synthetic, and dynamic statement. The modernity of the Theatre of the Grotesque is its ability of locating and identifying the multidimensional levels of the play; consequently, it has the capability of leading the audience to a level of consciousness where the subconscious and imagination is more likely to play an active role.

A fundamental component in Meyerhold's Theatre of the Grotesque is his work with "biomechanics." His emphasis on creating "the *jeu*" through a highly mechanical, constructivistic form of movement, patterns of which were systematically dictated by Meyerhold to his actors, does not lend itself to the dramatic form of realism and naturalism. . . .

Although *A Doll House* has its foundations in late nineteenth-century realism, Ibsen's use of symbol and Nora's archetypal pattern provide rich possibilities for a twentieth-century interpretation. Essentially it is this playwright's use of the symbol and the "child-archetype" motif that are the catalysts that unlock the complexities inherent in unconscious and collective thought. These early twentieth-century Russian theatre practitioners have within their ideology and technique the means to give shape to this dramatic vision. Whereas [director Konstanin] Stanislavsky's "psychological realism" is a fundamental interpretive approach to *A Doll House*, the ideals and the practices of the Theatre of the Grotesque establish a palette and a sense of style which are capable of revitalizing the psychological depths of the play.

A Doll's House Is Inconclusive

H. Neville Davies

H. Neville Davies, a fellow of the Shakespeare Institute at the University of Birmingham, explains that despite many critics' complaint that the conclusion to *A Doll's House* is inconclusive, the "dramatic pattern" of the play is in fact successful in its completion. Davies suggests that Ibsen's subplots in the drama, the stories of Linde, Krogstad, and Dr. Rank, give audiences the satisfaction of definite closure. Paired with these subplots—one of hope and one of hopelessness—Nora's story takes on new meaning. Her own life may hold either of these possibilities as she steps into an unsure future.

The thud of the street door closing behind Nora at the end of Ibsen's *A Doll's House* provides, as it must, an emphatic emblem of severance. Yet, in Adrian Noble's authoritative Royal Shakespeare Company [RSC] production, that resolute off-stage bang and Torvald's pathetic on-stage whimper conclude a play whose final impression is one of undogmatic openness. Ibsen's ending, so neatly reversing the Act I ringing of the door bell and the initial entry of Nora with her Christmas shopping, is a conclusion in which nothing is concluded, though a dramatic pattern is most satisfyingly completed. . . .

Earnest pre-performance programme readers nervously in search of guidance are . . . supplied with Ibsen's clearly conceived synopsis, entitled 'Notes on a modern tragedy':

> . . . The wife in a play ends by having no idea what is right and what is wrong; natural feelings on the one hand and belief in authority on the other lead her to utter distraction. A woman cannot be herself in modern society, with laws made by men and with prosecutors and judges who assess feminine conduct from a masculine standpoint.

Excerpted from H. Neville Davies, "Not Just a Bang and a Whimper: The Inconclusiveness of Ibsen's *A Doll's House," Critical Quarterly*, Autumn 1982. Copyright Manchester University Press 1982. Reprinted with permission of the author. Endnotes in the original have been omitted in this reprint.

She has committed forgery, and is proud of it; for she has done it out of love for her husband, to save his life. But this husband of hers takes his standpoint, conventionally honourable, on the side of the law, and sees the situation with male eyes.

Moral conflict. Weighed down and confused by her trust in authority, she loses faith in her own morality, and in her fitness to bring up her children. Bitterness. A mother in modern society, like certain insects, retires and dies once she has done her duty by propagating the race. Love of life, of home, of husband and children and family. Now and then, as women do, she shrugs off her thoughts. Suddenly anguish and fear return. Everything must be borne alone. The catastrophe approaches, mercilessly, inevitably. Despair, conflict and defeat.

Discussions of the play often begin with this text, or with its heading, but it is important to remember the status of the passage, as the RSC programme note admits by remarking that Ibsen composed his account before writing *A Doll's House*. It is, in fact, an *aide memoire*, never intended for publication, that records a primitive stage in the evolution of a play that changed profoundly as it was worked on. The value of the quoted passage lies, therefore, not in any appropriateness as an authorial preface to *A Doll's House*, but in its enabling us to see retrospectively how the play surpasses, even refutes the original simple conception. To apply the title 'Modern tragedy' (*nutids-tragedien*, literally 'contemporary tragedy'), as [critic] Muriel Bradbrook and others have, to the fully evolved play, is to overlook vital distinctions.

THE IMPORTANCE OF SUB-PLOTS

Conspicuously absent from the early plan is any mention of the two sub-plots—that concerning Dr Rank and leading to the conventional tragic conclusion, death; and that concerning Christine Linde and Nils Krogstad but leading to the conventional comic conclusion, marriage. These counterweights are carefully poised either side of a main plot, in which suicide is averted and a marriage fails. Thus a full spectrum is envisaged in the actual play. The contrasting sub-plots, with their complementary but alternative resolutions, suspended until just after the end of the action, present with schematic clarity the range of possibilities that life offers, and their stagey, melodramatic quality highlights the comparative naturalism and inconclusiveness of the central story.

The Christine Linde–Nils Krogstad plot takes the *confidante* and the villain from the main plot and combines them in a romantic sub-plot of their own. The story is an unlikely one. Years ago Christine rejected Krogstad's proposal of marriage, not because she did not love him, but because the responsibility of caring for an invalid mother and two little brothers led her to enter a loveless marriage with a well to do businessman. She allowed Krogstad, then an impecunious clerk in a solicitor's office, to believe that she had no feelings for him, in order to ensure the end of their relationship. That husband is now dead and his business has failed, leaving Christine a destitute and childless widow without even the satisfaction of needing to work to provide for her family, the mother having died and the brothers having grown up. Krogstad's life is also in ruins. Following the trauma of rejection by Christine he went to the bad, married unhappily, destroyed his career by dishonest dealing, and is now a widower trying desperately to regain respectability for the sake of his children, though regarded as an outcast by former associates.

When, in the play, Christine and Krogstad come together again, they are granted, against all the odds, the miraculous opportunity of a second chance. The marriage they failed to contract all those years ago becomes a possibility once more, and this time there will be no mistake. The world of Ibsen's play, then, is one that does admit miracles, that genuinely countenances the notion of a second chance. The dialogue even stresses the point when Christine answers Krogstad's fear that she might be offering herself to him merely to rescue Nora: 'Nils, a woman who has sold herself once for the sake of others doesn't make the same mistake again'. In Ibsen's Norwegian the remark is generalised, since 'a woman . . . herself' is the translator's expansion of an unsexed pronoun. Torvald Helmer's earlier comments to Nora, explaining Krogstad's professional misconduct, had also allowed for the possibility of a fresh start: 'I'm not so heartless as to condemn a man for an isolated action. . . . Men often succeed in re-establishing themselves if they admit their crime and take their punishment'. And there, too, the remark is more general than the translation indicates: 'Men often' could well be translated as 'There are many who'.

If sub-plot is related to main plot, one marriage comes into prospect as another breaks up. But this reversal of fortune also implies that Nora's assertion, that 'the miracle of miracles would have to happen' before a true marriage could exist for her and Torvald, cannot entirely exclude such an eventuality. Even though Nora herself may no longer believe in miracles, Torvald's response, 'I want to believe in them', a more purposeful statement in the original language, counts for something; and, guided by the playwright, the audience can by this time draw on the evidence of the subplot's happy reunion. . . .

The bearing on the main plot of the fully worked out subplot is further enforced by parallels of circumstance and experience. Most obviously, Nora shares with Krogstad the crime of forgery, as well as a charge of corrupting her children by bringing lies and deceit into their lives. Equally significant, however, is the emphasis placed on the emptiness and wretchedness of Christine's life after her husband's death, a sobering glimpse of the sort of existence that Nora is to enter at the end of the play. If the sub-plot offers hope by showing that a lost marriage may be retrieved, even when a forger is involved, it also injects a chilling realism by fleshing out the implications of Nora's choice. In Act I Christine has told Nora that 'These last three years have been just one endless slog for me, without a moment's rest', though inept translation here makes a highly expressive evocation of the joyless life of a lonely woman struggling to survive sound like a routine, almost jaunty complaint. And, in the Act III scene between Christine and Krogstad, we are again reminded of Christine's solitary existence, 'so dreadfully lost and empty'. . . . Without an adequate awareness of what is in store for Nora (and Nora is much less experienced and capable than Christine) the significance of her final action would be trivialised to become merely a histrionically effective exit. . . .

DR RANK

Like the Krogstad–Christine sub-plot, Dr Rank's role was also not part of the original conception recorded in Ibsen's 'Notes on a modern tragedy'. . . . The simultaneous arrival of Mrs Linde and Dr Rank—they pass on the stairs—is a significant indication of paired or complementary functions, and this equivalence is accentuated by the coincidence of their illness (whether temporary or chronic), and by Rank's intuition that the newcomer, Christine, will supercede him in the Helmer household. Finally, in Act III, when the Helmers come home from the party, intrusive encounters with Rank (who now knows his fate) and Christine (who now knows hers) reaffirm the parallelism.

The 'miraculous' second chance of Christine Linde's re-union with Krogstad is balanced by the contrary experience of Dr Rank, a bachelor who is cruelly denied even a single chance. His life has been blighted from birth by the dissipa-tion of his father, and as Christine prepares for a second mar-riage he prepares for death. . . . In the fully evolved play, the three days covered by the action are as critical for Dr Rank as for anyone. During that time he is waiting for the results of the laboratory tests that will enable him to ascertain the hope-lessness of his medical condition. But equally hopeless is his love for Nora, the unattainable wife of his closest friend. When he declares his passion, he only succeeds in destroying the re-laxed companionship that he enjoys with her, and which means so much to him; and, ironically, makes it impossible for the woman he loves to enlist his aid when she most needs it. The nearest Rank comes to consummating his passion is when Nora teases him with a pair of her flesh-coloured silk stockings, as they sit on the sofa together, in a dimly lit room. The episode is a poignant revelation of desire unsatisfied, an episode that entered the play only after the draft had been completed. In fact, there is no indication whatever, in the draft, that Rank is in love with Nora. It seems, therefore, that the fashioning of complementary sub-plots, one offering new hope and the other no hope, to provide, as a context for the main plot, a world in which both miracles *and* disasters oc-cur, was a process that Ibsen felt his way towards very grad-ually. None the less, the Dr Rank sub-plot, which developed particularly late, is related to the main plot by additional par-allels of circumstance and experience just as effectively as is the Christine–Krogstad sub-plot. Linking Rank and Nora is the important theme of hereditary weakness, and they share, too, a confrontation with death. . . .

THE INCONCLUSIVE CONCLUSION

The conclusion to the main plot envisaged in 'Notes on a modern tragedy' is 'Despair, conflict and defeat', but, by the time Ibsen came to write the scenario for Act III, Nora's role at the end had changed radically from a passive to an active one. After Torvald has emptied the letter box and gone to his room 'Nora, in despair, prepares for the decisive step; is already at the door when Helmer comes with the opened letter in his hand. Big scene. The door-bell rings. Letter to Nora from Krogstad. Final scene. Separation. Nora leaves the house.' This scenario remained the basis both of the draft and of the final version, though the famous thud of the door as it closes was a *coup de théâtre* not added until a late stage. From one point of view the play ends with the regrettable breakdown of a marriage; from another the ending presents an exhilarating escape from stifling constraints, and announces the start of a new life. These two view points are finely balanced, and in production neither should predominate consistently. . . .

Ibsen himself was particularly scrupulous not to impose authorial judgement, or make any final recommendation. The so-called serious discussion that precedes the separation rightly impresses audiences by its seriousness, and by the importance of the issues raised. On the other hand, its validity seems to be undermined by the dramatic context. The discussion takes place late at night when both participants are exhausted, and when they are both badly shaken by having just learned of the imminent death, under particularly distressing circumstances, of their closest friend, with whom they had spent a festive evening. Nora is in a highly disturbed state, having endured several days as a blackmail victim, and having come very close to suicide. Torvald, besides having to face the shock of Krogstad's letter, is sexually frustrated, his amatory advances having just been repulsed by his wife; and he is, too, decidedly the worse for drink. Were his drunken rudeness to Christine characteristic behaviour, he would never have been appointed to the position he now holds at the bank. Although their marriage may be such that, in normal circumstances, a serious discussion between Nora and Torvald could not have taken place at all, we recognise that decisions arrived at, and acted upon, under the extraordinary conditions of this particular discussion are open to question. But then there is no denying the impressiveness of the discussion itself. Ibsen, who was a dramatist not a polemicist, has balanced the negatives against the positives with consummate skill. And even if the unpropitious circumstances are overlooked, it is not easy to express a preference, if the choice has to lie between Nora's selfish egoism and Torvald's hideous self esteem. . . .

The fact is that Ibsen's main plot is unresolvably inconclusive. It ends with a question mark, and the two sub-plots, which do not end inconclusively, point in opposite directions. Adaptations, like Ibsen's own alternative ending, reluctantly written for the German theatre, which has Nora relenting when Torvald compels her to see the sleeping children before leaving; or [movie director Rainer] Fassbinder's depressing conclusion in which Nora also stays, though there are no children . . . or the very free adaptation by [playwrights Henry] Jones and [Henry] Herman entitled *Breaking a Butterfly,* in which a British Torvald (rechristened Humphrey Goddard) instantly takes responsibility for his wife's forgery; all of them are, in Ibsen's phrase, barbaric outrages.

Ibsen's Victorian Audience

Tracy C. Davis

Author Tracy C. Davis of the Northwestern University School of Speech, takes an original look at Ibsen by analyzing his Victorian audience rather than the plays themselves. Despite negative reviews for *A Doll's House*, Victorians flocked to the play to see what all the fuss was about in the press. These varied crowds were made up of people from all economic classes and professions. Early Ibsen critics scorned the Ibsenites, the fans that filled the theater night after night, and often directed as many negative comments to the theatergoers' style of dress or their poor behavior as they did to Ibsen's dramas.

In recent years, Victorian criticism of Ibsen has been collected and analysed, but until now the composition and behaviour of Ibsen's audiences have not been considered. Because his plays were the mainstay of the original London fringe, the patrons' identity and their artistic tastes are important indicators of the popularity and financial viability of alternative theatre in late–nineteenth century London. Anti-Ibsen critics repeatedly asserted that Ibsen did not pay, that he was not popular (*ergo* he was unsuccessful), and that his adherents should give up trying to tout him, but other evidence about the productions of 1889–1896 shows that there was a limited popular audience of greater size and diversity than anti-Ibsenites reported.

In the 1880s, the efforts of a few British critics and translators generated interest in Ibsen among some intellectuals, socialist activists, and university students, but until Walter Scott's Camelot edition of 1888 made three prose plays (*The Pillars of Society*, *Ghosts*, and *An Enemy of the People*) available for a shilling, Ibsen was not controversial among or ac-

Excerpted from Tracy C. Davis, "Ibsen's Victorian Audience," *Essays in Theatre*, November 1985. Reprinted by permission of the author. Notes and references in the original have been omitted in this reprint.

cessible to a wide readership. Once Ibsen had been widely read, an unadapted theatrical production was feasible. The reading public is significant: by the end of 1893, more than 31,000 volumes of Ibsen's plays had been sold in England (the first edition of Shaw's *Quintessence of Ibsenism,* in contrast, sold no more than 2,000 copies in six years). This gave English readers evidence with which to judge continental enthusiasm; most important, it sparked interest in a full trial, on stage, with a professional cast, and an uncut, unadapted translation.

Charles Charrington and Janet Achurch instigated the trial when they undertook to present *A Doll's House* in June 1889. They were neither Ibsenite idealists nor visionary reformists—in all likelihood, they probably only wanted to recover pledged property before embarking on an antipodean tour—and there is no evidence that they expected or even hoped to run the play for longer than a week. They hired the obscure Novelty Theatre in Holborn, scraped together a functional set (with Norwegian dressings by William Archer), and advertised Ibsen's "domestic drama in three acts" for seven performances.

This was a demure beginning, and a genuine test of Ibsen's attraction for a theatre audience. At the first performance, attendance was not large, and neither the fashionable first-nighters nor "the rowdy element customary on such occasions," was present. This production, like all later Ibsen ventures, attracted the favourably-partisan playgoers "who have been practically driven from the other theatres by the intolerable emptiness of the ordinary performances." No one (not even Archer) had dared to hope *A Doll's House* would be a popular success, but apparently the first night crowd was so enthusiastic and the vast majority of theatrical reviews were so negative that on subsequent nights the 556 seat theatre was filled again and again with playgoers trying to find the truth of the matter. The enthusiasm and controversy generated during the first week convinced the managers to extend the run by a fortnight. *A Doll's House* drew about 14,000 spectators in three weeks and Archer was delighted to pronounce it "the great event of the week—almost of the season. It has been more talked about and written about than even *The Profligate* [by Henry Arthur Jones]. It holds the great B.P. [British Public] like a vice—and what's more, they pay to see it.". . .

Judging from hundreds of comments by reviewers, actors, producers, and spectators, I estimate that in 1891, forty-eight performances of five Ibsen plays attracted about 26,000 spectators, and that, in addition, thirty-two performances of two Ibsen parodies (*Ibsen's Ghost* and *The Gifted Lady*) played to over 19,000 people. These numbers represent a very small percentage of overall London theatre attendance—even of overall West End attendance—and a trifle of London's total population of four million persons, but Ibsenites did not aspire to compete with the mainstream, or hope to provide a mass entertainment. Ibsen attracted people who were interested in contemporary literature (whether or not they had literary aspirations themselves), publicity-seeking socialites, genuine devotees of the drama and acting, and ordinary playgoers whose curiosity was raised by the plethora of press attention.

IBSEN'S PLAYS DRAW VARIED CROWDS

First night critics of the 1889 *Doll's House* were confident that it would not appeal to "ordinary playgoers," but devout Ibsen worshippers could not have taken every seat every night for three weeks. A commentator in the *Pall Mall Gazette* discovered "some poor and common enough people in the pit," and W.B. Yeats remarked on a middle-aged washerwoman who sat in the gallery. Undoubtedly, a few playgoers went in complete ignorance of what they would see— Yeats's washerwoman, for example, probably expected a pantomimic entertainment suitable for the young child accompanying her, and by the middle of the first act she had realized her mistake and departed. Of those who went deliberately and who stayed to the end of the play could be found people of all classes, from all walks of life, and with all degrees of literary sophistication. Within days of the première, anti-Ibsen critics were grumbling about the dramatic "craze" of Ibsenism that had set in among a claque of "faddists"; it is probably reasonable to suggest that the "Ibsen faddists" were as much a mixed sort of people as the Ibsen audiences.

Nevertheless, anti-Ibsenites insisted that the spectators at Ibsen performances of the late 1880s and early 1890s were social misfits, led by depraved tastes to seek the obscure and undesirable in art. Thus, the enthusiastic reception given some plays was only to be expected from "a scant audience

of unnatural-looking women, long-haired men, atheists, so-
cialists, and positivists, assembled . . . to gloat over the Ibsen
theory of women's degradation and man's unnatural su-
premacy.". . .

Attendance at all theatrical performances was affected by
the drawing power of the actors and plays involved as well
as by the reputation of the theatre performed in. No one theatre was devoted to Ibsen's plays, and Ibsen producers only
temporarily reclaimed houses from burlesque, farce, and
comedy. . . . Early Ibsen producers preferred afternoon performances, hoping to attract the "trial matinée" audience,
and of course, to avoid the financial risks of an open-ended
evening run. But the hour of performance (as well as the
month) affected the numbers able to attend, and as long as
Ibsen remained in the matinée bills, he was protected from
"the great practical ordeal of the play-house," which was the
submission to "'the tumultuous judgment of the pit.'"

Certainly at Ibsen matinées, the pit and gallery audiences
were not the customary proud enthusiasts led by [theatrical
critic] Clement Scott to value respectable, decorous plays of
limited realism. According to Jacob Grein, the pit and upper
boxes housed Ibsen's greatest fans: those whose creed was
"the play's the thing" and who cared little for scenic splen-
dor. The "Captious Critic" went to the pit and gallery to discover what Ibsenites were really like:

> Never before, except at an entertainment for the mentally or
> physically afflicted . . . had I encountered so many deformed
> faces; so many men and women pale, sad-looking, white-
> lipped. It was like an assemblage of outpatients waiting for
> the doctor. I seemed to feel in the midst of unhealth, chronic
> feebleness of the body, which could expect no help from the
> brain. . . .

EARLY CRITICS SCORN IBSEN'S FANS

The majority of critics were predisposed to disliking Ibsen,
and this is reflected not only in their judgements of the plays
but also of the Ibsenites who praised them. A *Pall Mall Gazette* reporter observed the critical fraternity at work on his
first visit to *A Doll's House:*

> I sat in the stalls, surrounded, I suppose, by the elite of the
> London press. Early I became aware that these gentlemen as
> a body held a brief for Society. They were solicitous about its
> foundations. They had come prepared to defend those objects
> of solicitude at any sacrifice—even of critical coherence. A

A DOLL'S HOUSE CONTINUES TO INSPIRE REFORM
Robert Ferguson notes in Henrik Ibsen: A New Biography
*that some contemporary Islamic groups have adopted Ib-
sen's play as a tool to reform sexual relationships.*

As an attack on marriage *A Doll's House* is no longer of relevance for the grandsons and granddaughters of those for
whom it was written. Separation, divorce, children who grow
up recognising one, three or more parents are commonplaces
of western society. On the other hand it has propagandic relevance for societies aspiring to reform the terms of the sexual
relationship. It has acquired notable appeal for advocates of
an Islamic reformation, and has twice in recent years been
performed in Oslo by visiting and native Islamic theatre
groups. An adaptation of *A Doll's House* has also recently been
the subject of an Iranian film.

stern championship of the Home, the Hearth, the Family, glit-
tered cold in every eye; nor was I reduced to gathering this
purpose from silent indications. They stirred, they hemmed,
they *snorted*. They pronounced expletives and protests. "Morbid stuff," "Dull twaddle," "Call this a play?"—these were
among the more articulate manifestations. In a word, these
gentlemen were plainly bent on asserting, either the superi-
ority of their morals, or else the inferiority of their manners.
Next day I looked for the morning papers with interest, and
read their comments without surprise. So much for the first
night in the critical stalls.

The reporter was able to attend again, in an unofficial capacity. In another section of the house he discovered quite a
different response:

On the other occasion I went to the pit. Never was a greater
contrast. A mixed lot of people they were, some poor and
common enough. But all keen, struck, attentive; sympathetic
and curious by turns. At the stage where the Press had failed
any longer to contain itself, the Public became more than ever
all eyes, all ears. Questioning there was, no doubt, a mood of
puzzlement and challenge. But stupidity and ear-stopped cla-
querie, none. A drunken man or so, perhaps—otherwise
nothing akin to the atmosphere of first-night criticism.

Irrespective of personal bias and specific complaints arising
from the moral and technical innovations of the plays, most
playgoers were fascinated by Ibsen, as Scott discovered at a
revival of *A Doll's House:*

It was curious . . . to watch the effect of the first dose of Ibsen on
a singularly attentive and intelligent audience. As the sermon

proceeded—it is not a play—the close observer could almost feel the impression made on the varied minds of the spectators. The sceptical opened their mouths and swallowed it as if it had been manna from the dramatic heavens; the religious scoffed at it; the matter-of-fact exposed its astounding fallacies and nudged their neighbours to emphasize their convictions; the serious opened their eyes at it, and the witty likened it to the extravagant satires of Swift or the methodical dramatic topsy-turviness of W.S. Gilbert. This remark has not been made before to our knowledge. . . . But let the truth be told. The play swayed and interested the audience to an individual. The novelty of the new dramatic religion was so astounding that people of all creeds sat still and opened their eyes. . . .

The dramatic revolution and renaissance predicted by the early Ibsenites did not come about, and as long as Ibsen was not popular, his detractors insisted that he could not be regarded as absolutely successful. His importance was overlooked by the majority of playgoers, who never ventured into a private or suburban playhouse. A mass audience simply had not been generated by the end of the nineteenth century. Beyond the Stage Society, few English producers dared professional productions of Ibsen or his followers and little headway had been made to establish a popular yet serious drama for the audience that had seen Ibsen at the Vaudeville, Royalty, Terry's Opera Comique, and Haymarket in the early 90s. A limited audience meant limited runs, usually only one or two performances, usually by amateurs. Between 1900 and 1920, the longest-running Ibsen production was Ellen Terry's *The Vikings* (1903), with thirty performances—Mrs. Patrick Campbell's celebrated *Hedda Gabler* (1907) was seen at only seven matinées. Compared to this record, the pioneering productions (including [Janet] Achurch's 1889 *Doll's House* and [Elizabeth] Robins's *Hedda Gabler, The Master Builder,* and *Little Eyolf*) were long-lived, popular, and financially viable enterprises that attracted Victorian playgoers of all classes and persuasions.

Ibsen's Contribution to Realism

J.L. Styan

J.L. Styan, professor of English literature at Northwestern University, discusses how Ibsen puts as
much effort into the realistic representation of Nora
as he does expressing the theme of women's rights
in the play. Nonverbal details help to build Nora's
character throughout the play; she does not need inflated language to seem real to the audience. Styan
writes that the challenge for actresses playing such a
real character is that they need to be both mentally
and physically talented, passing realistically from
"gloom to gaiety and then to dignity" as the play pro-
gresses.

A Doll's House (1879) is almost as topical today as it was a
century ago, as [modern] revivals have shown. Yet even today's critics, like those of the nineteenth century, fail to remark the play's extraordinary technical achievement, because its explosive subject matter is still so obsessive that no
room seems left for objective appraisal—a point well made
by Michael Meyer in his indispensable biography of Ibsen. If
we are overwhelmed by the theme of women's rights and the
concept of a woman's duty to herself rather than her self-
sacrifice in marriage, perhaps we should be as impressed by
the fact that Ibsen had also visualized his Nora right down to
the 'blue woollen dress' she wore. He championed the character quite as much as the cause. Of course one must ask
why it was that no one could be untouched by the play: but
was it only the issue of female emancipation and the relentless slamming of the door with which Nora walked out of
Torvald Helmer's life, the whole sensational package, which
made this play a masterpiece? Few of these effects would
have been felt so strongly had not the quieter strategies of Ib-

Excerpted from J.L. Styan, *Modern Drama in Theory and Practice*, vol. 1, *Realism and
Naturalism*. Copyright 1981 by Cambridge University Press. Reprinted with the permission of Cambridge University Press.

sen's work prepared for them: in the several revisions of the play Nora's character grew more and more subtle in an increasingly rich subtext.

In her 1928 lecture to the Royal Society of Arts, *Ibsen and the Actress,* the American actress Elizabeth Robins argued that in his script Ibsen actually 'collaborated' with his actor. She cited the moment when in *The Master Builder* Hilda sat on a little stool at Aline's feet and hugged her knees on the line, 'Ah, here one can sit and sun oneself like a cat', and she observed how the warmth and sensuousness of those words were set in contrast with her chilling statement a moment later, 'I have just come up out of a tomb'. When Robins played Hedda Gabler later, she remarked Ibsen's 'supreme faculty of giving his actors the clue—the master-key', for she had felt Hedda 'warm to my touch' and, in spite of Hedda's repellent qualities, saw her as 'pitiable in her hungry loneliness'. 'Make no mistake', she concluded, 'you must let Ibsen play you, rather than insist on your playing Ibsen'.

Although the perceptive George Moore, like other commentators who could not forget the shocking message of *A Doll's House,* found the play 'wooden', 'hard' and 'illogical', no actress playing Nora then or now could fail to be struck by the number of nonverbal details with which Ibsen built up her character: at the opening of the play, Nora's joy in her Christmas tree and the presents she has bought, the toys for the children; her extravagant tipping of the porter; her pleasure in her macaroons and the childlike way she eats them, hiding the bag from Torvald and surreptitiously wiping her mouth; her act of taking the money from him, and then pulling the button on his coat for more. The business of the macaroons and the money was added in the final version, and is a clear indication that Ibsen knew he was creating a particular life, and making sure that his actress could enrich her performance by working with such details. Nora's games with the children are nicely held in reserve as a foil for the sinister entrance of Krogstad; although this was possibly a retreat towards the melodramatic, it was also a device by which the whole situation was embellished in order to dramatize Nora's two lives. The earlier version omitted the second-act Christmas tree; in performance, it stood there stripped of its ornaments, looking bedraggled, its candles burned down, lending a special atmosphere to the stage. In this act Ibsen also added the flesh-coloured stockings with which Nora flirts with Dr Rank, and at the end of this act, when Nora must distract Torvald from finding Krogstad's incriminating letter, Ibsen substituted for the Turkish dance to Anitra's song from *Peer Gynt* the new symbolism of the tarantella, danced wildly to a tambourine by Nora with her hair fallen loose. And in the third act, this immodest wife of a sedate bank manager wears her Neapolitan costume with its large black shawl in order to continue the exotic image of the tarantella—all this before she changes, symbolically again, into her drab, everyday clothes in preparation for her shattering final exit.

ADAPTATIONS AND TRANSFORMATIONS OF *A DOLL'S HOUSE*

Yet even the reader for the Royal Theatre, Copenhagen, which first staged the play, found Nora's action in walking out psychologically 'unsatisfying', and there were not many like the reviewer for *Folkets Avis* of 24 December 1879 who noted its unusual economy of method and its absence of blood, tears and other melodramatics. There is a minimum of inflated language at the end of *A Doll's House,* and it ends promptly when its point is made. The play offered a true advance in style, but it was its content which provoked outrage and hostility. For the German production, Ibsen was compelled to write a so-called 'happy ending', lest it was rewritten without consulting him: the German ending has Nora, torn between her wish to leave her husband and her urge to stay with her children, merely sink to the floor. It is as significant that, at a time when Ibsen's name was a household word throughout Europe, the play did not appear on the British stage for ten years, or on the French for fifteen. Indeed, the play's adventures in the English-speaking world imply a total distrust of its theme. America saw a first English production in Milwaukee in 1882, and this was an emasculated version by W.M. Lawrence entitled *The Child Wife.* In 1884, London was treated to Henry Arthur Jones's adaptation of the play into an English setting, entitled *Breaking a Butterfly;* in this, Torvald became Humphrey, Nora became Flora or Flossie, and, needless to say, Humphrey and Flossie were tearfully reconciled at the fall of the curtain. In 1885, London also saw a limping amateur performance in aid of none other than the Society for the Prevention of Cruelty to Children. In one translation by a certain T. Weber, Nora's famous curtain line became, 'That cohabitation between you and me might become a matrimony!', and [play-wright Harley] Granville-Barker was so struck by this that he thought a prize should be given at the Royal Academy of Dramatic Art to the student who could say the line without making an audience laugh.

London had to wait until 1889 for a fully professional pro-duction. This was by Charles Charrington at the Novelty Theatre, Kingsway, in William Archer's translation, with Charrington playing an icy Dr Rank and Charrington's wife, Janet Achurch, aged twenty-five, playing Nora, the first great Ibsen part seen in Britain. It was played, in the eyes of Eliz-abeth Robins and her friend Marion Lea, to 'a sparse, rather dingy audience' in a 'pokey, dingy theatre'. The production caused the expected stir, and apart from one or two enthusi-asts like William Archer and George Bernard Shaw (who was yet to deliver his Fabian lectures on Ibsenism in 1890), it was generally condemned as an example of a morbid and perverted new cult concerned with the degradation of women. It was at this time that Clement Scott, writing in *The-atre* on 1 July 1889, was the first to use the word 'Ibsenite' as a term of opprobrium. Again, any technical achievement in the writing or the acting went unnoticed, other than *The Times*'s facile condemnation of the play's 'almost total lack of dramatic action' and *The People*'s decision that the infamous ending was not only immoral, but 'essentially undramatic'. It was as yet too soon for the general audience to change its way of seeing, and if it did not find the play positively ob-scene, it found it dreary.

We turn to Elizabeth Robins for any comment on the per-formance. She was impressed by the 'unstagey' effect of the whole play: it was less like a play than 'like a personal meet-ing'. How refreshing it was to see Achurch break the rule that a leading actress must always enter in new clothes! She struck a note of gaiety and homeliness: 'You saw her biting into one of the forbidden macaroons, white teeth flashing, blue eyes full of roguery.' She was particularly impressed by Nora's 'warm bright confidence splintering against that tombstone of a man'—Dr Rank. Only the tarantella seemed to be a piece of theatricalism, 'Ibsen's one concession to the effect-hunting that he had come to deliver us from'.

The London production went on tour, arriving in America in 1895. New York audiences applauded Achurch's Nora (as they were to applaud the French Nora, Gabrielle Réjane, in the same season). . . . The conception of the new woman lay not merely in recognizing her intellect and independence; she was also required to perform in a new way. Audiences had only to compare the excessive emotionality and resonant tones of the girl Margrete in Ibsen's *The Pretenders* of 1863 (with lines like 'Respect a wife's grief!' and 'Blessed be your mouth, even though it curses me now!') with Nora and her richly observed detail of speech and behaviour, to see that the two belonged to different worlds.

THE ACTOR'S CHALLENGE

William Archer was among the first to recognize that Nora's actress needed to be especially talented mentally and physically. In *The Theatrical World* for 1893, he reported that he had seen the Italian Nora of Eleonora Duse at the Lyric Theatre, and approved her 'spontaneous, effervescent, iridescent' gaiety of the first act. But he found her less satisfying than Achurch, and his reasons are some of those by which naturalistic theatre may be judged. Duse had failed to respond to certain loaded words which called for a more *subtle* reaction from the actress, as when Krogstad told Nora that her father appeared to have signed the note of hand three days after his death, and again when Torvald suggested that Nora should admit the guilt she knew was really hers. Archer also found that Duse failed to perceive the *hidden rhythm* of the second act, which passed from gloom to gaiety and then to dignity; she had instead painted the whole scene in one colour. But he surprisingly approved her decision to cut back the tarantella, which he too thought was 'Ibsen's last concession to the old technique' and 'beneath her dignity', even though he appreciated a comparable contrast between the Capri costume of the last act and Nora's death-like, ashen face as she wore it.

As time passed, comments of a more technical kind were heard. Writing in *The Saturday Review* of 15 May 1897 about a new production of *A Doll's House* at the Globe Theatre, London, Shaw was able to make a comparison with what he had seen eight years earlier. He found Courtenay Thorpe's Torvald 'overwhelming' for being spoken with genuine feeling: 'We no longer study an object lesson in lord-of-creationism, appealing to our sociological interest only', he said. But Shaw also observed that some of Torvald's more fatuous lines were still uttered as 'points', thereby destroying their realism. (A 'point' in the Victorian theatre was a striking moment in performance when the actor revealed an essential element of character or situation by emphasizing a special piece of business or by speaking a line in an arresting voice; Victorian actors acquired their reputations by punctuating their performance with as many points as possible.) In the production at the Globe, Achurch had revived her memorable Nora, but she replaced the wide-eyed naïveté of her former youthfulness with a less girlish sophistication. For the 1890s, these were all fine considerations in performance criticism, and Shaw concluded his notice by remarking, 'The flattering notion, still current in the profession, that anybody can play Ibsen, is hardly bearing the test of experience.' . . .

IBSEN THE REALIST

Ronald Gray has recently thrown doubts upon the claim that Ibsen was a master of realistic portrait painting. In *Ibsen—A Dissenting View* (1977), Gray accuses the playwright of having sacrificed character to plot, reducing Torvald in *A Doll's House,* for example, to a stereotype of a Victorian husband as a way of justifying the excessive gesture of Nora's decision to leave him. . . . It is possible to multiply instances which suggest that Ibsen allowed his plots to determine his characterization, and it is certainly a good thing to examine propositions that are normally taken for granted. Yet these arguments are of the closet, and Ibsen in performance is another matter. Degrees of 'realism', of what seems real, change from age to age, of course, but the quality of enduring realistic detail in a characterization may be tested only in performance over a period of time. . . . The truth seems to be that Ibsen's lines do embody characters who possess all the qualities and dimensions necessary to fashion a great individual performance. We are in an especially good position today to verify the enduring elements in Ibsen's characterization, since we are sufficiently remote from most of the limiting social concerns of his first audiences, which made [a] sinner of Nora . . . and [a] saint of Torvald.

CHAPTER 2

Nora

READINGS ON
A DOLL'S HOUSE

Nora's Awakening Self

Lou Salomé (Siegfried Mandel, translator)

Professor Siegfried Mandel of the University of Colorado, author of numerous books and articles in comparative literature, translates the work of Lou Salomé. A contemporary of Henrik Ibsen and friend to such famous figures as Rainer Maria Rilke and Sigmund Freud, Salomé was once described as "the most intelligent of all women" by Friedrich Nietzsche. Here, Salomé discusses the development of Nora Helmer, the heroine of *A Doll's House*. While Nora is seemingly happy playing the role of her husband's "little lark," Salomé suggests that, from the start, the potential for conflict is brewing under the surface of the couple's childlike love. Having had a taste of independence while working in secrecy, Nora's character develops more fully when her secrets are exposed and she chooses to leave her husband and children.

Upon her first appearance, [Nora] is laden with shrouded holiday parcels; surrounding her deepest conflicts and dreams are secret festivity and presents. With a trustful and childlike anticipation of twilight, she awaits a wonder.

Christmas is a children's festival, and Nora is a child. Her childishness creates her charm, her danger, and her destiny. As the sole daughter of a widower who in his carefree ways spoiled her instead of bringing her up seriously, Nora grew older only in age. The transformation from her carefree days as a girl to marriage meant no more to her than a change from a small doll's house to a larger one; the main difference was that instead of her customary lifeless wax dolls, she would eventually receive three precious living dolls.

She brought her accustomed love for both play and parent to her marriage with Helmer; it was a love developed in the relationship between daughter and father—devoted, sin-

Excerpted from Lou Salomé, *Ibsen's Heroines*, edited, translated, and with an introduction by Siegfried Mandel (Black Swan Books, 1985). Reprinted with permission from Limelight Editions, Proscenium Publishers, Inc.

cere—in which she looked upward with the open-eyed adoration of a child. . . .

This childish innocence and inexperience permits her to assume without question that her husband embodies everything that is good and noble, as does a father in the eyes of a child. And so, courtship and marriage must seem to her a superabundant gift which one is obliged to accept thankfully and uncritically; it is also a mysterious and precious gift, toward which one is led blindfolded, with good manners. She is overwhelmed and can hardly grasp the magnitude of the gift, the love offering. For the husband who towers so high above her has not only inclined himself to give fatherly solicitude and accustomed sustenance, but out of his free choice has elevated her to be his wife, to be one with him. It seems to her like an incomprehensible miracle, and she believes in it as a child would. With this sense of the miraculous there awakens in her for the first time a new, exclusive world and a development—a world of humility and pride; an unconstrained giving of herself to her husband; together with the first stirrings of her search for self-identity and worth. The first impulses of her slumbering strength are awakened; instinctively she attempts to come into her own in order to be capable of making a yielding gift of herself. Her slumber is dissipated by anticipatory dreams of a true marriage. . . .

She remains in her small, circumscribed world of play and vanity. High and remote above arches a sky of miracles, and its infinite blue she sees joyously reflected in humans and things. Though distanced from reality, she gradually senses that her relationship with Torvald Helmer is that of a charming child to a parent, and not one of equals. Yet, ever more patiently, she looks for a miracle from above.

"I have waited," she says toward the end, "so patiently for eight years; God knows, I realized quite well that wonderful things cannot come as daily commonplaces." Helmer has no inkling of her expectations. Nothing lies farther from his mind than changing their relationship; in no way does he share Nora's need for self-fulfillment, equality and mutual growth. At the core, she remained childlike, while he was a self-satisfied adult. The wish for growth is a child's pleasure that trustingly demands self-transcendence. For Helmer, that would be as unwelcome as outgrowing accustomed clothes. . . .

CONFLICT BREWS BENEATH THE CHILDLIKE LOVE

Nora's love is at home in some wonderland, while his is anchored in his doll's house. Childlike love entwines itself, like a vine, on the lover, and negligently the toys and dolls of earlier years fall from her hands. The self-satisfied and assured adult, who has no one to look up to, deliberately chooses for his love-object a toy or doll for the idle hours between important business. He chooses a "squirrel" that can perform tricks when he is bored; a "skylark" that can sing away a sour mood; and a "nibbly cat," made sufficiently happy by proffered candy during a light mood. Content with himself and Nora, he smugly says, "I do not want you to be anything but what you are, my lovely, dear little skylark."

It really does not occur to him that it was his love that gave impetus to her development and the extension of her life's horizon, with intimations of something infinite. His sealed doll's house does not lend itself to disruptive change; it must retain his sense of comfortable order. Love in the doll's house cannot be expansive, but can only be added to with gay decorations. Helmer loves the picture of Nora happily humming as she strews the Christmas tree with colorful strips; that, he feels, is her true mission in life. Nothing warns him that the childish birdsong warbling from her lips bridges over into a silent hymn of a blessed—but vain—expectation of a Christmas miracle whose flame can only be lit by him.

Nora does not know that love and beauty have opposite meanings for them both. She does not yet know that Helmer's delight in simple gaiety and loveliness is, at the same time, a conventional person's reluctance to face any serious struggle which could disturb the aesthetic somnolence that allows him to enjoy life with self-satisfaction. It is not without reason then that Doctor Rank, the sick friend of the family, avoids having Helmer attend to him during his struggle with death. He knows that Helmer has "a pronounced repugnance to anything which is ugly." And not unfittingly is the turn in Nora's destiny entwined with Helmer's in the profound struggle that ensues. The view he offers her turns her love into death.

The apparent moral strength that Helmer fosters, his need to appear above reproach and to retain his dignity without stain, all the self-control evidenced in his daily life, is rooted in a central egotistic pleasure-seeking. On the obverse side, however, there is an unmistakable sign of petty fears—the fears of a human to engage in conflict. The contrast between Nora's naïve judgments, undisciplined inclinations, and inherited disposition to frivolity and lavishness, and Helmer's correct bearing and rectitude most surely intimidate Nora. Appearances are deceiving: his self-satisfaction is disguised by a serious moral mien, while her deep-slumbering seriousness constantly seems to be transformed into a joyful child's face.

Sometimes she is provoked and tosses a lightning expletive into Helmer's nice, tidy, carefully constructed world. And it only takes a stressful situation to produce involuntary quarrels that stem from her actions. Long before their inner differences become evident to her, the seeds of conflict are sown by the many outer dissimilarities between care-free inexperience and well-cultivated strictness. . . .

A TASTE OF INDEPENDENCE

[When Nora secretly works for money she claims,] "It almost seemed to me as if I were a man!" . . . Strength and independence slowly unfold secretly and grope toward release. Although she is left in the dark and enmeshed in a network of lies, there comes the first unconscious expression of protest against her father and husband, both of whom have kept her in bondage to childishness and ignorance. But protest does not surface in her consciousness; on the contrary, she does not wish Helmer to take notice of her awakening self. A fine, feminine instinct decidedly tells her that she must keep the charm she possesses in Helmer's eyes; her naïve love-charms are poised against the sounder, stronger and more intelligent man. It is no dissimulation when she looks up to him with love and admiration. Her childlike façade, that hides much from others, is for Helmer no masking but the visage of true and humble love. With indignation, Nora rejects the advice of her childhood friend, Mrs. Linde, that she confess everything to Helmer, although Nora herself had confided her secret to Mrs. Linde, herself an experienced and diligent person, in order not to appear flighty. . . .

Despite her hard-won and blissful independence, she does not in the least wish to play her trump card against him and change her admiring glances into the bold ones of an equal partner. It is not the sobriety of a strenuously won equality that she sees in her dreams of a true marriage; she seeks instead the miracle of an incomprehensible love that draws her upward toward him and increases in wonder the higher he, a god, towers over the child. The only value she places on her actions and intrinsic worth is that they derive from her love. She excludes any thought that ultimately he could be displeased or indignant at the secret life of her last eight years.

She sums up that life in her confession: "I have loved you above everything in this world!" One cannot work for, nor earn, a miracle. It must surprise one, as does grace, spirituality, poetry. But in nothing do the energetic uniqueness and the urge for completion within her awakening individuality express themselves more clearly than in her recognition that expectation, longing, and trust must willy-nilly be transformed inwardly into creative action. She is not content to let the Christmas mood take its course, but she participates in the pleasure of preparing Christmas gifts. She works at her love-offering for Helmer when she strives to free herself; yet she wants to achieve her freedom only to make him a present of it. In darkness, secrecy, and behind closed doors it originates, destined to be among the Christmas gifts. That makes her proud and happy, expectant of a transformation.

The appearance of her old friend, Mrs. Linde, casts a harsh and sober pall over Nora's festive joy; Mrs. Linde resembles the hard workday—cold, joyless, and as grubby as her relentless work for bare necessities. The prohibition of every outer luxury, of everything that could be done without, constricted and oppressed Mrs. Linde's inner life; the potential richness of her nature was emasculated, and only utilitarian and sensible considerations found expression. Long ago she turned her back on the practicing lawyer Krogstad, a man she loved, and contracted a marriage that made the financial support of her [family] possible. And after a sad and bleak marriage, her husband died and left her nothing—not even a child to care for. Now she offers Krogstad her hand in order to save him from the shipwreck of his existence. From her bitterness and loneliness she gathers whatever resources her heart once possessed, and she seeks one last, modest luxury within the long, tiring workdays of her life: *not* to work only and alone for one's bare necessities. Nora, on the contrary, draws this culminating conclusion from her marriage: "I have responsibilities to myself alone." That precisely was the most burdensome of all responsibilities for Mrs. Linde, and from which she now wishes to free herself at all cost. Nora later directs her gravest reproach against her husband's sealing her off from life, seriousness and experience, while Mrs. Linde, amid her coarse and lonely wanderings, searches for only one thing—a last, though modest, refuge from the battles of existence, which would house her love and care. . . .

NORA'S GUILT EXPOSED

At the moment that Mrs. Linde sees her old friend, Krogstad, he is about to use Nora's forgery of her father's signature on the bond as blackmail against Helmer who has dismissed him from his minor clerical post at the bank. Only desperation drives Krogstad to such a step; for the sake of his motherless children, he must retain his hard-won place in society. He himself was outlawed by society for similar forgeries in his devious business dealings. Mrs. Linde's determination to marry him and be a mother to his children has an ennobling, mellowing effect upon him. The unexpected gift of trust and friendship awakens his good qualities, whereas his former friend, Helmer, in a short time will prove himself to be a selfish coward with regard to Nora's great love and trust. Helmer is a weakling whose only concern is with his reputation in society. In Krogstad's happy desire to again be worthy of his lover, he stands as high over Helmer as does Mrs. Linde over Nora, in respect to patience, experienced goodness, and maturity. And so, Mrs. Linde's words, "we need each other," initiate the life of a true marriage, despite struggles with inevitable problems, while Nora's dream about her marriage and belief in the integrity of her husband collapse.

Krogstad's threat to tell Nora's husband everything and to note that the bank director's wife is guilty of the same type of forgery that he himself had committed earlier, makes Nora aware for the first time of her endangered position. She now realizes that she is a guilty party in the eyes of the law. But she is even more disturbed when she hears from Helmer about the aversion inspired in him by a man like Krogstad who has committed a misstep without atoning for it; how such a person creates a corrupt environment, and how he spins a web of lies in which his children must grow up. Nora' s fears rise and her well-kept secret no longer is a source of pride but an oppressive burden on her conscience. . . .

In stark contrast to her powerful mood, she is busy preparing for a masked ball, as the fateful letter from Krogstad is dropped into the mailbox of the house. While rehearsing steps for her dance, a *tarantella*—she tries to distract Helmer's attention from the letter.

In her efforts to seem unconcerned, Nora's usual frivolity bursts into abandoned and feverish wildness. What has matured and moved her far beyond the childish and the playful, she can only hide behind a mask in painful costuming. And so, her married life with Helmer expresses itself in an impromptu near manic performance of a studied dance, which

---

LINDE AND KROGSTAD

Although the majority of critical works about characters in A Doll's House *focus on the development of Nora, Linde and Krogstad are also significant characters in the play. As Harold Clurman writes in* Ibsen, *they represent mutual compassion and understanding and the potential for a true and happy marriage.*

Few people who see the play acted grasp the full significance of Krogstad's and Mrs. Linde's presence among the personages. They appear auxiliary to the main theme rather than part of it. Krogstad is the "menace," Mrs. Linde is Nora's friend and Krogstad's redeemer. But Ibsen has placed them prominently in the picture to suggest that they will make a truer marriage than was possible for Torvald and Nora. Krogstad's struggle to sustain himself as a man who has been all but ruined by adversity and poverty, his having been forsaken by Mrs. Linde, the woman he loved, the effort to support his children while he finds himself deprived of the possibility of decent employment, will ultimately prove the ground for renewed strength. Mrs. Linde's hardship, her loveless marriage to assume help for her mother and two brothers, lends her the fortitude to enter her future relationship with Krogstad on a basis of mutual compassion and understanding. They are equal in their experience of life's trials. Krogstad, albeit "shipwrecked" and desperate, manifests a stern practicality of behavior; Mrs. Linde throughout remains staunch and, as she says, unhysterical. They know themselves in all their missteps and in their situation in society. That is why their relationship eventuates in a "happy ending." It is also to be noted that Mrs. Linde believes that if Nora were to reveal her intention to her husband, their marriage would be "saved," that is, resurrected on a firm basis of truth.

he watches with harmless pleasure. Nothing warns him that this display of charm, this ultimate childlikeness, represents precisely the mere appearance of a boundless love, costumed for him yet one more time on her deathlike journey—while secretly she has readied a sober dress for a long wandering.

Helmer sees only the attractiveness of this love which lies intoxicatingly over her silent farewell. Champagne has roused his senses and stimulated desire for his wife. The words with which he pictures his intoxication are the replete expression of the poetry that streams from Nora to him, as well as of the worthlessness of his character which cannot cull anything deeper from such a love than a captive ornament for his comfortable existence. Delirium and love therefore dissipate as rapidly as does the champagne's inebriation. The letter lies in his hands. With tortured fright he is seized by the fear of the consequences of Nora's past actions on his behalf. In manic anger, he heaps scorn upon Nora and casts her out from his heart—but not from his home, because he wishes to keep appearances up for the sake of outsiders.

For Nora, things collapse; she feels as if the world were suddenly godless. Silent and petrified she stands before Helmer. What had remained to be taught her of cares and experience, now is completed in one instant: she suddenly sees life as it is, in the shape of Helmer, a conventional, pained person who is saturated with fear and selfishness. All her life and attentiveness has been focused on him. Since her life was sustained by *his* truth and interpretations, only through *him* could her life be shorn of God and thus destroyed. Even if her maturity had grown equal to the experience of this hour, her childlike heart in its depth retained faith, and her life its wonders. Even if everything else—independence and personal growth—lay waiting in anticipation, this new and singular situation launched her emancipation.

NORA'S NEW STRENGTH

And in the midst of Helmer's outbreaks of fear and anger comes Krogstad's second letter, accompanied with the bond, written in the mellow mood of his new-found happiness. "I am saved!" is Helmer's first outcry, "Nora, I am saved." Quietly she asks, "And I?" Obviously, she too is saved. And now, in a new light, she is clear about her situation and their relationship. With one blow, her moral indignation evaporates. Helmer sympathetically acknowledges her struggles and assures Nora of his willingness to forgive her. Indeed, he finds her doubly touching in her inexperience and helplessness; he assures Nora that her weakness endears her to him all the more because he can serve now as her strength and support to protect and guide her.

To Nora, it seems that she had been reduced to a lapdog which was whipped and then restored to grace, or that she had been treated like a doll which one discards and then picks up at the dictate of whim. With terrible and blinding clarity she becomes conscious of the fact that she had been a life-long toy and that she had lost her dignity in accommodating herself to others. Something strange and immeasurable changes her make-up. Her slowly awakening strength and independence—everything she had so humbly and busily gathered together for the gift of love she was going to bestow from her integral inner humanity—now rears up and wrests itself free in enormous protest. And so, a new, strange, strong human being is born, no longer kneeling nor enslaved nor able to be deceived.

And what has silently and overwhelmingly developed now finds expression. Awakened and without chains, Nora stands before Helmer and declares her freedom, simply, clearly, unconstrainedly. To the objections of an experienced and cautious mind, she seems naïve and still childish, but her unimpeachable, forward-looking, magnificent naïveté penetrates to the heart of things. . . .

And so, we leave Nora at the entrance into the unknown vastness of life, which opens darkly. Nothing as yet tells her if she will find a way toward her goal. No longer is the blue, arched sky comforting and enveloping. It is far and remote, and separated seemingly by immeasurable distances from the ground upon which she stands lost. Far, far at the horizon's outermost bleakness, there is a thin line wherein heaven and earth flow together within the ken of the human eye, promising reconciliation. With every step toward the horizon's line, what seems ideal recedes, and yet one journeys into the endless.

Despite such premonitions, a calm and dominating force within her courage and faith impels her to overcome Helmer. The masculinity and conscientiousness of her childlike persistence render Helmer's weapons—experience and insight—

useless. In the midst of his self-awareness and contentment, he strangely senses a secret power to which he must bow. Helmer, who had looked down upon Nora with considerate condescension, finds himself responding humbly to the determination of her childlike idealism, with this promise: "I have the strength to become someone else."

Nora Is Multidimensional

Sandra Saari

Sandra Saari has been secretary of the Ibsen Society of America since its founding in 1979 and is a professor of literature at Rochester Institute of Technology in New York. In this selection, Saari compares Ibsen's early drafts of *A Doll's House* with the final version to show how Ibsen's characterization of Nora changed as his work on the play progressed. Among other things, Ibsen chose to make Nora dance the tarantella instead of a slave-girl dance as originally planned, and his draft revisions take pains to paint Nora as a rational woman instead of a hysterical one. Both choices help to create a character that is recognizable and sympathetic not just as a woman of her times, but as a *human* of any time.

Ibsen's notes [for *A Doll's House*] outline the conflict between two kinds of moral law and conscience, between the feminine, with love as its highest value, and the masculine, with its social and legal moorings. The conflict leads to depression and loss of faith on the part of the female. The notes conclude grimly: 'desperation, struggle, and destruction'.

Although Ibsen wrote nearly an entire draft based on this idea of a feminine soul destroyed by a masculine world, it turns out that he never did end up completing that play. During his eleven months of writing in Italy, something happened. The vision Ibsen had recorded so clearly in his notes and had worked out so carefully in much of his Draft became radically transformed. Rejecting the concept of two mutually unintelligible kinds of conscience segregated by gender, Ibsen ultimately embraced an entirely different fundamental premise. Retaining a female protagonist, he created a play based on the premise that, though they tradition-

Excerpted from Sandra Saari, "Female Become Human: Nora Transformed," in *Contemporary Approaches to Ibsen*, vol. 6, edited by Bjørn Hemmer and Vigdis Ystad, Universitetsforlaget (Norwegian University Press), Oslo, 1988. Reprinted with permission from the author and publisher. Endnotes in the original have been omitted in this reprint.

ally inhabit different realms of the social and legal world, males and females demonstrate no essential difference in their spiritual makeup. . . .

THE MEANING OF THE DANCE

Visually, the most striking change from the Draft to the Final Copy occurs in the dance scene that marks the climax of Act 2. Krogstad's blackmail letter revealing Nora's secret loan and forgery is in the mailbox. To prevent Torvald from reading it, Nora distracts him. In the Draft she sings a song, then dances a shawl dance; in the Final Copy she dances the tarantella. In both the scene serves the plot function of postponing the crisis. However, in terms of characterizing the relationship between Torvald and Nora, the scenes differ dramatically.

In the Draft, as Torvald heads toward the mailbox, Nora strikes familiar chords on the piano. Beguiled by the promised recital, Torvald equips himself and Rank with 'genuine Turkish cigarettes', then sits back to bask in Nora's rendition of homage to male magnificence—her singing Anitra's song from *Peer Gynt.* This song from Act 4 celebrates Peer as the holy Prophet himself. Sung by Anitra, a dancing slave girl, it begins:

> His steed is like milk, the purest white,
> That streams in the rivers of Paradise.
> Bend your knee! Cover your face!
> His eyes are stars, tender and bright.
> No child of clay can endure
> The rays of their heavenly fire.

The text elaborates this visionary appearance of the male whose brilliance so bedazzles the mere female mortal that her eye is incapable of beholding it. . . . Singing this, Nora gives explicit voice to the theme of the male as lord and master of the universe, whose wisdom and dominion are absolute and to whom the female owes grateful and adoring devotion. . . .

Nora then dances with shawls. Torvald the connoisseur remarks to Rank, 'How lovely she is, Rank. Look at the delicate bending of her neck. What grace in her movements, and she is unaware of it.' Torvald takes aesthetic pride in this beauty of his, displaying Nora as his art object. Nora's lack of self-awareness, and thereby lack of self-possession, serves to increase his pleasure by increasing his definitive ownership. Underscoring this exhibition's being solely for male apprehension and appreciation, Nora comes over and, like a good little child, asks, 'Did you enjoy it?' 'Was it pretty?' Anitra's song and shawl dance in the Draft reinforce in verbal and visual terms the characterization of the relationship between husband and wife. Torvald is the all-knowing, adult authority figure, Nora the unself-possessed and adoring child.

As opposed to dancing attendance upon Torvald, in the Final Copy Nora does not sing and dance graceful obeisance. She dances the tarantella, a dance of her own self-expression whose increasingly wild execution displeases Torvald mightily. Far from beguiling Torvald by celebrating a hierarchical male-female relationship, the tarantella incenses Torvald by its abandon and deviation from his careful teachings. The folklore about the tarantella dance links it with the spider's poisonous bite, as either a cure or a consequence. Similarly in the play, the dance is the visual bodying forth of the fear of impending death that Nora cannot confide to anyone, but that she tries to stave off. The tarantella also serves as the first point in the play where Nora does not heed, at least in some superficial way, Torvald's commands. Unable to exert any direct control over her, he finally commands Rank to stop in order to force Nora to stop. With absolute bafflement he says, 'I would have never believed it. You have forgotten everything I taught you.' Exactly the opposite of reinforcing their hierarchical relationship, the tarantella is the visual embodiment of Nora's response to a reality that lies completely outside Torvald's tutelage. . . .

THE HYSTERICAL FEMALE BECOMES RATIONAL

Ibsen's most thorough-going and profound conceptual transformation from the original notes and Draft to the Final Copy is manifested in the shift of Nora's fundamental essence from female to human. In the Final Copy, Nora is 'first and foremost a human being'; her actions, thoughts, and ideals are *not* gender specific.

Of the three major changes in the characterization of Nora, the most obvious is the elimination of her hysterical 'female' behavior. In the Draft, Act 2 is replete with Nora's increasingly distraught behavior as she is caught between Krogstad's blackmail threat if he is not reemployed and Torvald's refusal to reinstate Krogstad. Not knowing where to turn, she appeals to a higher power for a miracle: 'Oh God, oh God, do something to change Torvald's mind, so he won't provoke that horrible man. Oh God, oh God, I have *three little children*. Oh, do it for my little children's sake.' Her behavior displays a desperate distraction at the thought of her husband's learning the truth. She goes out to get some fresh air; within seconds she comes back, saying that she couldn't stand to stay out, that she had been overcome with such anxiety. Repeatedly she starts off to see the children, then stops in mid-step. She tells Rank about being so horribly full of anxiety as to be in complete confusion. With suicide in mind, she frantically denies thoughts of not being with her husband and becomes terror-stricken at the thought of not seeing her children grow up. She listens at the door, desperately trying to hear what Torvald and Rank are saying about her. Act 2 culminates with Nora keeping Torvald from the mailbox by threatening to jump out of the window. On the basis of this irrational, hysterical behavior, Torvald and Rank conclude, not surprisingly, that Nora is mentally ill. All the overt symptoms are there in the Draft. They are all eliminated in the Final Copy.

The second major change in the characterization of Nora is the addition of rational purpose to her childish behavior towards Torvald. Although the frequency of her wide-eyed, simple-minded behavior increases from the Draft, in the Final Copy these incidents are deliberately childish in order to conceal or to ingratiate. From the outset, Nora's lark-twittering, squirrel-frisking, carefree behavior is rendered less monolithic in the Final Copy by the addition of the concealed macaroons. In the Draft, Torvald chides Nora for frittering away even the money she earned at copy work. In the Final Copy, he patronizingly teases her about the cat having destroyed her efforts at surprise Christmas decorations; that in actuality she had been doing paid copy work is a depth he doesn't perceive. Nora, on the other hand, perceives very clearly in the Final Copy the depth of Torvald's male egotism and acts to safeguard it. Early in Act 1, she explains to Mrs. Linde why he hasn't been told of the loan: 'Torvald with his manly pride—how embarrassing and humiliating it would be for him to know that he owed something to me. It would entirely disrupt the relationship between us; our lovely, happy home would no longer be what it is now.' In the Draft, like a child hiding something certain to anger the parent, Nora had concealed the loan because Torvald 'is so strict about such things and more than anything else in the world hates to be in debt'. Understanding, in the Final Copy, that he needs to feel completely in power, Nora employs deliberately childish behavior to wheedle Torvald, on-stage, into giv-

ing Mrs. Linde a job at the bank. In the Draft, she had 'pestered'
him off-stage. Her feigned incapacity to conceive a mascarade
costume adds yet another display of helplessness, which again
she assumes to maneuver Torvald into a good mood, the better
to entreat him on Krogstad's behalf.

That Nora in the final Copy is fully aware of her practised
self-effacement is evident in the exchange about Torvald's
solution of the Neapolitan fisher-girl costume:

> TORVALD: Yes, wasn't it a pretty good idea on my part?
> NORA: Marvelous! But wasn't I also good to give in to you?
> Torvald: (*taking her under the chin*): Good—because you give
> in to your husband? There, there, you crazy little thing, I
> know perfectly well you didn't mean it like that.

In spy-story terms, Nora has nearly 'blown her cover'. She is so
desperately anxious to ingratiate herself with Torvald, in order
to make him receptive to her renewed pleading for Krogstad,
that she inadvertently lets slip a clue to her own inner identity.
Because it is so discontinuous with his understanding, Torvald
discounts the clue as meaningless. But it corresponds perfectly
to the self-awareness Nora has already revealed to Mrs. Linde:
that someday Nora might tell Torvald her big secret, that she
borrowed money and thereby saved his life, someday, 'many
years from now, when I am no longer as pretty as now. Don't
laugh at that! I mean, naturally, when Torvald no longer feels
as good about me as now; when he no longer gets pleasure
from my dancing for him and my dressing up and reciting.
Then it might be good to have something in reserve.' Though
naturally she would not like to think that the day of Torvald's
lessening interest would ever come, nevertheless she takes
comfort in having the 'insurance' of a heroic deed with which
to counteract such an eventuality. Given her capacity to measure present actions against future outcomes, Nora is obviously
not to be confused with 'the elfin girl dancing in the moonlight'
that she tells Torvald, in the Final Copy, she will play for him.
Far from the irrational, hysterical Nora of the Draft, the purpo-
sive Nora of the Final Copy deliberately adopts a childish and
self-effacing posture towards Torvald in order to achieve her
goals. The depth of Nora's revised character reveals a discern-
ing and rational adult.

NORA'S HUMAN CONSCIENCE

The third, and by far the most significant, change in Nora's
characterization involves the identification of her thoughts

and ideals as human rather than feminine. Whereas in the Draft Nora had a specifically feminine conscience, in the Final Copy the makeup of Nora's conscience is in its essence the same as that of the male characters. This change is brought about primarily by additions and alterations to the secondary male characters.

In the Final Copy, Nora's suicidal thoughts are the result of human, not feminine, desperation. Ibsen inserts a lengthy dialogue that explicitly establishes, not merely the similarity, but the actual identity, of Krogstad's and Nora's desperate thoughts.

> KROGSTAD: —Therefore, if you are coming up with one or another wild resolution—
> NORA: So I am.
> KROGSTAD: —if you are thinking of running away from hearth and home—
> NORA: So I am!
> KROGSTAD: —or you are thinking of that which is worse—
> NORA: How did you know that?
> KROGSTAD: —then give up such thoughts.
> NORA: How did you know that I am thinking of *that?*
> KROGSTAD: Most of us think of *that,* at first. I thought of that too; but, Lord knows, I didn't have the courage—
> NORA: (*flatly*): I don't either.

In the Draft, Krogstad's suicide thoughts were dispatched in a single contemptuous speech: 'Bah, your life, your life. I also thought it was a matter of life and death when it caught up with me—but you can see for yourself that I lived through it.' The lengthy, point-by-point comparison of sympathetic dialogue in the Final Copy intertwines the male and female thoughts into a double-stranded chord of interwoven human despair. Though they are fierce antagonists, Nora and Krogstad reach a momentary communion on the basis of their common human experience.

Nora's ideas of love and death are likewise not characteristic of gender. Ibsen's radical alteration of Rank's function in the play—from being Torvald's confidant in the Draft, to being Nora's closest friend in the Final Copy—serves to establish Nora's conception of these fundamental issues as a human conception. Whereas in Act 2 of the Draft, Nora is filled with revulsion and leaves within seconds of hearing about Rank's impending death, in the Final Copy Nora, not Torvald, is the comforter to whom Rank confides his imminent doom. In Act 3 of the Draft, Nora is the mute onlooker while Torvald and Rank discuss Rank's dying. In the Final Copy, the uncomprehending Torvald impatiently waits to be alone with Nora, while Rank and Nora talk of laboratory tests and mascarades. Torvald's patronizing remarks, 'Just look; little Nora talking about scientific investigations!' and 'You little frivolous thing,—are you really thinking about the next one [mascarade] already!', demonstrate with dramatic irony his lack of awareness of the approaching death of his boyhood friend. That these remarks are completely disregarded by Nora and Rank serves to underscore in the strongest possible manner their sustained empathetic reverie on the human confrontation of personal death. Rank's revised function as Nora's 'closest and truest friend' allows her thoughts and comprehension of death to be portrayed as fully human.

Facing death is but one of the understandings of human experience shared by Rank and Nora. The other, more important in terms of the play, is love. In terms of the shift in Nora's characterization between the Draft and the Final Copy, this is Rank's most critical specific function in establishing Nora as a human being. In the Draft, Nora's concept of losing one's life for love is consigned to females and fantasy. Rank discounts as mere words Nora's idea that Torvald, in his love for her, might not withstand losing her: '. . . in most cases, something being the death of someone is in reality only a figure of speech, at least as far as men are concerned.' When Nora declares that she must perish, because otherwise Torvald will, Krogstad brusquely responds, 'I don't believe in novels', thereby assigning her idea to a fictional world. Nor does Torvald say anything in the Draft that would indicate that he ascribes to such a concept. Nora's conception of love as the ideal for which one would lose one's life is not a view of the real world from the male perspective in the Draft.

BELIEVING IN LOVE

In the Final Copy, love as the highest ideal is ascribed to by males as well. Torvald verbally embraces this ideal several times, the most memorable recital of which occurs in Act 3: 'Oh, Nora my beloved wife; I feel I can't hold you close enough. You know, Nora,—many times I've wished that an impending danger would threaten you, so that I could risk life and limb and all, all, for your sake.' Such an explicit statement gives Nora the resolution to have him read Krogstad's blackmail letter. Moments later, however, Torvald's actions reveal that this was sheer rhetoric, that preservation of public image is by far the higher value for him, and that, when he is at risk, such lofty sentiments are mere empty, foolish phrases.

It is Rank who provides the confirmation that Nora's conception of love is not simply a construct of the feminine mind, but is to be taken seriously as a human ideal. In the Final Copy of Act 2, Torvald cuts off Nora's entreaties for Krogstad's reinstatement with the reassurance that whatever happens, he, Torvald, 'is man enough to take everything on himself'. Nora, horrified, interprets this as Torvald's willingness, out of love, to sacrifice his career and reputation to save her. Though earlier she had been entertaining thoughts of running away to avoid poisoning her children, she now sees that she must at all costs prevent Torvald's self-sacrifice. She is galvanized to action. Far from hysterical, she conceives of a rational solution to Krogstad's blackmail: she will pay off the loan and thus retrieve the forged note.

Despite his announcement of imminent death, Nora approaches her friend Rank with the intention of asking for the money that would prevent Torvald's self-sacrifice:

> NORA: You know how wonderfully, how indescribably much Torvald loves me; never for a moment would he hesitate to give his life for my sake.
>
> RANK: (*bending toward her*): Nora,—do you think that he is the only one—?
>
> NORA: (*with a faint start*): Who—?
>
> RANK: —who would gladly give up his life for your sake.

Since moments later Rank states explicitly that he loves Nora, it is not to avoid that overt statement that Ibsen has Rank repeat Nora's phrase. By reiterating, 'who would gladly give up his life for your sake', Rank gives witness to love as an ideal for which a male is prepared to give his life. In the Final Copy, Nora's highest value is not a mere figure of speech in the male world. Ideal love is a shared, supremely valued concept of the human conscience for Nora and Rank.

By her actions, Nora immediately testifies to the strength of this ideal of love. Interrupted by Rank's profession of love, Nora abandons her intention to ask him for the money, despite his repeated requests to be allowed to do her a favor. She tells Krogstad that she has no solution for obtaining the money that she 'chooses to make use of'. She finds instead the courage to choose suicide.

In his first notes for the play, Ibsen conceived of the conflict leading to complete confusion and finally to destruction. In the Final Copy, the conflict leads to Nora's clear, rational perception of reality and consequently to her rejection of the child-wife role. When the miracle doesn't happen, Nora is no longer willing to base her actions toward Torvald on the ideal of love. From the beginning of the play, Nora perceives that Torvald has faults such as egotism and jealousy, but, understanding that 'miracles don't happen every day', she discounts these faults as being superficial, not essential. There is good reason for her to interpret them thus. Torvald describes himself as having great inner strength in a crisis, and he explicitly espouses love as his highest value.

In the Draft, Nora says Torvald forfeited her love when she saw that he wasn't better than she was. In the Final Copy, she says he forfeited her love when the miracle didn't happen. 'The miracle', the approach of which Nora had already announced to an uncomprehending Mrs. Linde in Act 2, has the ring of unrealistic fantasy. But it is, in fact, a further development in the Final Copy, of Nora's ability to see things in a rational and ordered manner. What she means by 'miracle' is: an action in the real world that confirms beyond all doubt her belief that their marriage is based on the shared ideal of love, in particular, that Torvald loves her, as she loves him, above all else, above even life itself. When the miracle doesn't happen, when what happens is instead a disconfirmation of her belief, then she relinquishes her belief. . . .

At the end of Act 2, Nora had 'danced herself free', to use Daniel Haakonsen's felicitous phrase, in response to a reality that didn't conform to Torvald's instruction. At the end of Act 3, Nora has rationally thought herself into freedom from Torvald's interpretation of reality. She then sets out to define reality for herself. . . .

The last part of Act 3 bears a close resemblance to the Final Copy in its basic conception of Torvald and Nora. When, in the Draft, he penned Nora's words, 'I believe that I am first and foremost human', Ibsen had virtually arrived at his final conception. In revising, he had only to make her declaration even more explicit: 'I believe that I am first and foremost a human being, just the same as you are.'

Nora as Rebel

Declan Kiberd

Declan Kiberd, author of *Synge and the Irish Language,* writes that Nora's inclination toward rebellion against her doll-like existence, though suppressed, is inherent in her character early in the play. Though she is ignorant of laws, she is conscious of her role as a child-wife and unsatisfied that her marriage is based on lies and fiction. While she waits, like a child, for miracles on the one hand, on the other, she is eager to act out of emotion for the good of herself and others. Finally, when Torvald acts to forgive her crime and welcome her back under his protective wing, she rebels against him and his dollhouse, sickened by the lack of equality that continues to dwell there.

[James Joyce writes:]

Ibsen's knowledge of humanity is nowhere more obvious than in his portrayal of women. He amazes one by his painful introspection; he seems to know them better than they know themselves. Indeed, if one may say so of an eminently virile man, there is a curious admixture of the woman in his nature. His marvellous accuracy, his faint traces of femininity, his delicacy of swift touch, are perhaps attributable to that admixture. But that he knows women is an incontrovertible fact. He appears to have sounded them to almost unfathomable depths. . . .

Ibsen's account of the sufferings of couples who reject the stereotypes of masculinity and femininity, only to face more daunting social and personal problems in their attempt at an honest sexuality, seemed to Joyce *the* central issue of the age. The radical critique of bourgeois marriage in *A Doll's House* was a challenge to its own generation. . . .

'You are totally unaware of the spirit which prompted him', said Joyce to a friend in defence of Ibsen. 'The purpose of *A Doll's House* for instance is to further the emancipation of the woman, which is the most important revolution of our time because it concerns the most important relationship possible—that between the man and the woman.'. . . [However,] near the end of his career, Ibsen reprimanded the extremists of the Norwegian Society for Women's Rights: 'I am not even quite sure what women's rights really are. To me it has been a question of human rights. . . . Of course, it is incidentally desirable to solve the problem of women.'. . .

LIFE IN A DOLL'S HOUSE

As an artist, Ibsen's aim was to reverse the process of a law which, in the words of Krogstad, does not investigate motives—and to examine just those motives from the female standpoint. He realised that men and women are a lot less alike than the law pretends, and a lot more alike than the culture admits. The challenge was to make the law as androgynous in its world-view as art, so that it recognises *all* the faculties of the human mind, the 'natural feelings' of the female allied to the male belief in 'authority'. The man who lives only by authority, like the woman who lives purely on feelings, can never be whole. Hence the two-dimensional character of Helmer is not a flaw in Ibsen's dramatic technique, but part of the play's psychological point. Helmer has projected all the emotional aspects of his personality on to Nora, the doll-wife, who in turn projects all her own childishness onto her 'doll-babies' that 'dogs never bite'. At the end, it is her fear that she will perpetuate those values if she does not leave: 'But our home's been nothing but a playpen. . . . I thought it was fun when you played with me, just as they thought it fun when I played with them. That's been our marriage, Torvald.' Helmer's hypocrisy is manifest. He treats his wife like a juvenile and then complains when she acts like a child, making noise or scoffing macaroons.

The free woman who walks out in the finish is latent in Nora from the outset, in her private commitment to the male values of work as well as to the female code of self-sacrifice. Faced with the financial stringencies of the previous Christmas, she locked herself in a room making decorations. To Helmer's complaint that it was the dullest time he ever lived through, Nora brightly responds that it wasn't at all dull for her. In those late December nights, she had a rare sense of self-sufficiency and learned the joy of 'being' rather than 'having'. The greatest threat which Nora now faces is Helmer's new-found affluence which will deny her the few remaining opportunities for being and instead compel her to become the full-time female fetish of his possessive dreams. The macaroons will ruin her white teeth and rotten teeth will not excite him. 'You wanted so much to please us all', drools Helmer, who has trained Nora in the art of self-censorship, so much so that she is surprised by her repeated candour in the presence of Mrs Linde ('thoughtless me, to sit here chattering away' or 'I'm talking of nothing but my own affairs'). Family life has surely threatened her selfhood, just as it jeopardised the life of her husband, who overworked to the point of serious illness in order to support the couple in their early days. In his permanent obsession with letter-writing, bank business and work, Helmer is as much a victim of a specialist code as his wife. Every major play by Ibsen foretells the death of the family as an institution based on a false specialism of roles, man for work, woman for the home. . . .

That Nora is not the doll she impersonates is clear from the beginning. It is the suppressed adult in her who complains that everything seems so ridiculous, so inane. She may be ignorant of her disadvantages under the law and have to be told that a wife cannot borrow without her husband's consent, but she is all too well aware of the discrepancy between her assigned role and her real contribution in the home. She has kept the secret of how she borrowed money on false pretences to save Torvald's life, because she understands the fiction on which the family is based. . . . She jokes of deliverance from her debt by an admirer of her beauty, but in the end it will be necessary for her complete freedom that she walk out to an uncertain future without even that consolation. She is fully conscious of her role as child-wife, enacting for a prosaic husband all the playfulness he has learned to suppress in himself. Her secret may well have the coercive power of this manipulation in years to come when she is no longer attractive. . . . She knows just how precarious is an institution which is based more on a youthful figure than on a spiritual affinity. The fact that all the other marriages mentioned at the start are hollow mockeries is scarcely encouraging. So already, even in her attempts to save her own marriage and defray the awful debt by extra work as a copyist, Nora is half-consciously preparing for the moment of self-support. 'But still it was wonderful fun, sitting and working like that, earning money. It was almost like being a man.' The masculine element is beginning to emerge not only in Nora's desire to say 'to hell and be damned' but also in Mrs Linde's successful usurpation of her former lover in his post at the bank. It is brutally appropriate that the undoing of Krogstad should be achieved by Nora's skillful playing on Helmer's vanity as a male—'she's terribly eager to come under a capable man's supervision'. . . .

WAITING FOR MIRACLES

One of the great achievements of this play is to suggest an underlying similarity between the plight of Nora as a woman and that of her blackmailer Krogstad as a criminal. He, too, uses his obligations to his own family as a licence for threats and deceit, just as Mrs Linde invoked her family as a justification of her cruelty to him. In such a context, Nora's final abandonment of the family as an institution may not be as shocking as it is sometimes made to seem. Her warning to Krogstad seems to hint at an identity in their predicaments: 'When one has a subordinate position, Mr Krogstad, one really ought to be careful.' This equation is underlined by Helmer's admonition that such a guilt-ridden one must always wear a mask, even before his own children. Nora's lifeless admission to Krogstad that she, too, lacked the courage for suicide suggests the kind of candour in their relationship which in her marriage itself would be as yet unthinkable.

At this early stage, as Ronald Gray and John Northam have argued, Nora has no vision of society as a whole. At the start, she told Helmer that if she died in debt, she would care little for the strangers to whom the money was owing. 'Just like a woman', he responded, but her reply showed a more fundamental, nonlegalistic intelligence: 'If anything so awful happened, then it just wouldn't matter if I had debts or not.' Now in Act 2 she still shows scant regard for the rights of strangers, when she wonders if Helmer could dismiss some clerk other than Krogstad. In this case, 'natural feelings' win out over 'authority', but in the case of her children, such is the force of 'authority' over 'natural feelings' that Nora loses faith in her own fitness to be a mother. All around her is the evidence of corruption by inheritance—in Rank's mortal disease, in her own amoral attitude to society—with the result that Nora cannot bear the thought of infecting her children. Mrs Linde stresses the positive elegance and charm in Nora's inheritance from her dead father, but the evidence is all against her. There is nothing left for Nora but to revert to the role of doll-fetish, amazing Helmer by rebellious irony ('But wasn't I good to give into you?'), or teasing Rank with the stockings which she snaps in his longing face. Such a scene proves that Nora is a doll only by curtailing her sensitivity to the feelings of others—that all too often manipulativeness is mistaken for femininity. It is at this unlikely moment, however, that Nora achieves an heroic self-sufficiency and rejects the easy option of having Rank solve her financial problems. She has manipulated him shamelessly, because that is her time-honoured role; but now, shocked at her own success in putting him into her power, a more honest woman emerges in Nora and steadfastly refuses to press her advantage home. She is angry at Rank not for loving her, but for telling of his love. When he asks if she knew all along, her reply works on many levels: 'how can I tell what I know or don't know?'. . . Nora's explanation is uncanny enough to convince Rank: 'there are some people that one loves most and other people that one would almost prefer being with'. As a child, she loved Papa but preferred the talk of the kitchen, on the principle, perhaps, that our servants do our real living for us.

Act 2 ends with Nora waiting for the miracle which will occur when her husband decides to take all the blame of her bad debt on himself. According to her idealistic plan, he will do this only to discover that she has already beaten him to it and taken her own life. The idea of an impossibly noble self-sacrifice seems to dominate every major character in the play. When Mrs Linde proposes marriage to the disillusioned Krogstad in the final act, with the explanation that there's no joy for a woman in working for herself, he suspects 'some hysterical female urge to go out and make a noble sacrifice'. But she has already made one sacrifice too many in sacrificing him. The woman who sold herself once, for the sake of a dying mother, won't (she assures him) do it again. Her homely realism, which admits its own selfishness, contrasts refreshingly with the rather unreal sacrifices preached, but not practised, by the others. Everybody, of course, has made sacrifices for the family, because those with nothing to live for are unspeakably empty. Rank is one such and he tries to retrieve his life by offering some great proof of his friendship for Nora. Even Helmer has delusions of melodramatic self-sacrifice, wishing to find himself in some terrible danger, so that he could risk his life for the sake of his wife. It is part of Nora's weakness that, far from seeing through such rhetoric, she should embrace it as her own. It is her last and greatest illusion of all, that Helmer will take on the guilt and shame. He would need to love her to do that, but all he loves are his reasons for loving her. The 'helpless' doll whom he loved is a fetish of his own creation, who now trembles as she dances the tarantella. The masterful woman who sought to influence his decisions at the bank or who rebuked him for pettiness is another proposition altogether and he bludgeons her into submission by a burst of anger and recrimination. Somewhere hidden in Nora was a real woman who for a while lived vicariously through her husband and found it 'amusing that we—that Torvald has so much power now over those people'. But now, as she dances the tarantella, the real priorities of Nora and her husband are laid bare, for in the mythologies of the world, the tarantella is a dance of androgynes, after which women behave like men.

Torvald has dressed Nora in a fishergirl's costume to gratify his fantasies, but also to display her beauty as his prized possession. He does not love her for herself, but for the sake of his own aggrandisement. Her performance of the tarantella was a little 'too naturalistic', but this is forgivable in one who 'made a success'. It was naturalistic because Nora was truly doing the dance of death, expressing at once her colossal vitality and the imminence of her chosen doom. Helmer is as unaware of this as he is of the forecasting irony of his next complaint about Nora's strange reluctance to leave the dance: 'An exit should always be effective, Mrs Linde, but that's what I can't get Nora to grasp.' He talks of Nora in the third person, as if she were a demented child with no mind of her own, and his relationship with her is the clearest indication that his life is conducted on modes of 'having' rather than 'being'. Flushed by champagne—which Nora, with uncharacteristic bitchiness, says makes him 'so entertaining'— he spouts about 'the beauty that's mine, mine alone, completely and utterly'. Mrs Linde's belief that Nora would have been wiser to tell her husband everything is now put to the test and found wanting. The same lady's decision to precipitate the catastrophe by not recalling Krogstad's letter is vindicated, however, in her own words: ' these two have to come to an understanding; all those lies and evasions can't go on'.

Helmer's explosion into recrimination, just after his prayer for the chance to sacrifice himself for Nora, is the deflation of her final illusion. There will be no miracle. With callous pragmatism he points out that her suicide would solve nothing. The only thing for it is to put up a brave front of domestic harmony, despite the fact that Nora will no longer be allowed to bring up the children. . . . It is presumably at this point that Nora realises that her dream of a noble suicide is entirely inadequate to the occasion. . . . A deeper question remains, however, about her own attitude to him. If Helmer were to shoulder the blame, the consequences for his entire family would be far more disastrous than if Nora were merely to plead inexperience. Such an act would be impractical as well as counterproductive. Moreover, it would offer just the kind of male protectiveness which Nora has found so nauseating in his performances.

THE DOLL'S HOUSE DISMANTLED

The myth of the 'helpless creature' is the one illusion which remains to be dismantled.

It is this very myth which Helmer hastily tries to reactivate, as soon as he learns that Krogstad has decided to show mercy. He reverts to it in his attempts to woo Nora back from the brink: 'I wouldn't be a man if this feminine helplessness didn't make you twice as attractive to me.' In the past, one of his favourite games was to smile at Nora across a crowded room, imagine that she was his bride-to-be and woo her all over again. Now, in a pretentious metaphor of forgiveness, he relaunches this fantasy: 'It's as if she belongs to him in two ways now; in a sense he's given her fresh into the world again and she's become his wife and child again.' Unfortunately for him, Nora by now has changed out of her fishergirl's costume and into her regular clothes, as if to suggest her rejection of her role as a fetish of the male imagination. It is the adult in her who now takes command and regrets that she has lived by doing tricks for him, without a serious discussion between them over eight whole years. The fault is not entirely his, of course, for in withholding her secret, Nora has shown a deep distrust of Helmer from the start. In playing the coquette so obligingly, and for so long, she has merely fed his foolish fantasies. It is he, rather than she, who is finally revealed as the perpetual child, unable to change or grow. . . . Helmer knew well that the woman he married had no sense of social responsibility, but he liked things that way, married to 'a wife and child'. It is this scenario which he tries to recreate in the closing scene: 'I'll be conscience and will to you both.' He does not try to educate her, preferring to find her ignorance charming. Rightly can Nora complain that her father and husband are to blame that nothing has come of her.

Lacking an education, Nora now advances a rational rather than a superstitious explanation of her rejection of her children. She cannot presume to teach them until she has first educated herself. Perhaps her departure is made easier by the knowledge that she is not giving up all that much, for in her stratum of fashionable society, elegant ladies were not only denied by their husbands the right to a job but were also denied by professional nannies the dignity of motherhood. If our servants are going to do our living for us, they are likely to make better mothers as well. Like many other Ibsen heroines, Nora grew up without a mother, but she leaves her children to her own nanny with the remark that they are in better hands than hers. The usurpation of the traditional female role of housekeeper and mother is admitted in Nora's assertion that the maids know how to keep up the house better than she does.

These remarks are all uttered with a staccato lucidity which gives the lie to those critics who feel that Nora is confused in this scene. She herself says that she never felt more clear-headed in her life. If anything, it is Helmer who grows confused, as his surface confidence evaporates and he tries to assimilate what is about to happen. Nora's first lesson is for him more than for herself:

HELMER: To part . . . I can't imagine it.
NORA: All the more reason why it has to be.

True education is about imagining future virtues, which will be admirable precisely because we cannot now conceive them. In a play where the word 'past' is interchangeable with the word 'guilt', the idea of an uncertain future has a liberating force, as much because it is uncertain as because it is the future. . . . But what if the culture and laws of the future were truly an androgynous blend of male honour and female love, to such a point that it became foolish to equate the one virtue exclusively with either sex? Then the living together of a couple would be a real marriage of minds, ful-filled in the very scope of their attributes. It is on this note of qualified optimism about the future of marriage that the play ends, a play which has already seen one good marriage con-tracted on the pragmatic understanding that is purged of all sentimental illusion. Ibsen has turned his suspicious gaze onto the institution of marriage, but has not yet given up all hope for its redemption.

[Playwright August] Strindberg denounced *A Doll's House* for its assault on the male and wrote off Ibsen as an 'igno-rant woman's writer' who had nothing to teach him. He in-sisted that Nora is a compulsive liar as well as a flirt, whereas Helmer is too honest a lawyer to plead for a shady client. This is untrue—Helmer's deal with Nora's father in-volved a technical dishonesty—and in the world of the emo-tions, it is he rather than she who lives a lie. Nothing daunted, Strindberg asserted that 'woman is in general by nature mean and instinctively dishonest, though we ruttish cocks have not been able to see it'. Nevertheless, he conceded that *A Doll's House* revealed marriage to be 'a far from divine institution', with the result that divorce between ill-sorted couples was increasingly considered justifiable.

CHAPTER 3

Women
in Ibsen

READINGS ON
A DOLL'S HOUSE

Marriage in *A Doll's House*

Otto Heller

Otto Heller, a professor of German language and literature at Washington University, writes that Ibsen's treatment of women in *A Doll's House* suggests his concern for the plight of women, and all individuals, in society. While critics condemn Ibsen for what seems an attack on the institute of marriage in the play, Heller notes that Ibsen's message is not that marriage is bad in and of itself, but that "matrimony should not be the end of freedom."

Personally, a writer could not well be farther from feminism than Ibsen was. A temperamental predilection for the feminine point of view is assuredly not one of his natural idiosyncrasies, and yet he became the most pronounced woman emancipator of the age. His indorsement of feminine claims is simply an act of unswerving allegiance to the force of logic. In many of his dramas a woman is the principal figure: Fru Inger, Helen Alving, Nora Helmer, etc., and in all his works such a prominent position is assigned to women that he has been universally applauded by the women's rights advocates. Yet when the Women's Rights League of Norway, at a general convention in 1898, extolled the poet's merits as a champion of their cause, he made the following characteristic reply:—

> I am not a member of the Women's Rights League. Whatever I have written has been without any conscious thought of making propaganda. I have been more poet and less social philosopher than people generally seem inclined to believe. My work has been the description of humanity. The task always before my mind has been to advance our country and give the people a higher standard. To obtain this, two factors are of importance. It is for the mothers by strenuous and sustained effort to awaken a conscious feeling of *culture* and *discipline*. This feeling must be created before it will be possible to lift the people to a higher plane. It is the women who are to solve the social

Excerpted from Otto Heller, *Henrik Ibsen: Plays and Problems* (Boston: Houghton Mifflin, 1912).

problem. As mothers they are to do it. And only as such can they do it. Here lies a great task for woman. My thanks; and success to the Women's Rights League!

Throughout his career [Ibsen] dreamed of the reorganization of society through woman. Addressing the workingmen of Trondhjem, June 14, 1885, he said:—

> The reshaping of social conditions, which is now under way out there in Europe, is chiefly concerned with the future position of the workingman and of woman. This transformation it is that I am awaiting, and for it I will and shall work with all my power as long as I live.

"A woman cannot be herself in modern society," says Ibsen, 'which is a society exclusively masculine, having laws written by men and judges who pronounce upon women's conduct from the masculine point of view." In a sketch for *A Doll's House*, Nora says: "The Law is unjust, Christine; one can notice clearly that it is made by men.". ...

The tremendous excitement aroused by *A Doll's House* ("Et Dukkehjem," 1879) was due to a habitual confusion. The criticism of marriage in the concrete was taken as equivalent to an attack upon the institution of marriage and a plea for its abrogation; no wonder men's minds were staggered. Was it not rather true that, as an ardent believer in the sacredness of marriage, Henrik Ibsen viewed with a sense of alarm the prevailing misconception of its meaning? He believed in the possibility of noble union between husband and wife, because he believed in woman. . . .

And yet the average masculine notion of a happy marriage and a perfect wife, at the time when *A Doll's House* was written, sadly discountenanced the requirement of spiritual companionship. Petty domestic tyranny was still in full blast. The Nora of the first part of the play, still more the Nora of the anterior plot, fairly represents the unspecified type of femininity then in demand for the purpose of marriage. Women themselves hardly ever called in question the sanctity, let alone the moral legality, of marriage between persons spiritually unrelated. They were not a little startled to see the marriage problem elevated to the foremost theme of dramaturgy by Ibsen, and to hear it reiterated, from *A Doll's House* to the *Epilogue*, that marriage can only be happy when it rests on the basis of common ideals; that only when a man and a woman have the will and strength to give and to take with equal measure may they merge their lives and be entitled to equip a new generation with the gift of life. In an age of enlightenment true wedlock should differentiate itself from illicit or ephemeral union of the sexes, in that the husband looks upon the wife as his peer and partner, entitled to share his anxieties and troubles as well as his successes. . . .

[In Nora, Ibsen imagines] a young and yearning creature, fairly willful and of stormy temper, grown up without the discipline of work and responsibilities, without as much as a single confrontation with any of the serious sides of life, and having basked perpetually in the fulsome adoration of parents and other admirers,—imagine her all of a sudden married. Married moreover to a man of sterling but chilly uprightness, whose heart is a walled fortress of the proprieties, whose ambition knows no goal beyond that of being a "mainstay of society," and whose highest satisfaction consists in the good opinion of the neighbors. How would such a woman bear herself in the crisis? Will her spirit emerge unshaken from the supreme battle for her liberty, against a form of oppression all the more dangerous for its remoteness from any outer baseness and brutality? For in *A Doll's House* we have to do with a type of egoist far more insidious in his virtuous serenity than was the criminally minded Consul Bernick [in Ibsen's *Pillars of Society*]. When Nora has disclosed her unalterable decision to part from her husband, she makes a memorable retort to his desperate plea.

> HELMER. This is monstrous! Can you forsake your holiest duties in this way?
> NORA. What do you consider my holiest duties?
> HELMER. Do I need to tell you that? Your duties to your husband and your children.
> NORA. I have other duties equally sacred.
> HELMER. Before all else you are a wife and a mother.
> NORA. That I no longer believe. I believe that before all else I am a human being, just as much as you are—or at least that I should try to become one.

How does Ibsen arrive at such a startling formulation of a world-old problem? In the posthumous writings the short notice on *A Doll's House* shows precisely how for him a problem springs into actuality. In the first sentence a poetic theme is stated, so to speak, *sub specie ærni*; Ibsen speaks of the eternal tragical antagonism between the masculine and feminine modes of life and thought. In the second paragraph the problem is narrowed down to the domestic sphere, and in the third the woman question as it is to-day is touched.

By wresting speeches like the above from the context it was a simple matter for prudery, whether attired in petticoats or in trousers, to distort and misstate Ibsen's main argument. Nora's declaration of independence, when unintelligently garbled out of every logical coherence, cannot but go counter to the religious interpretation of woman's duty, likewise to the well-nigh universal sentiment of husbands. A great hullabaloo was raised about the poet's ears by the Amalgamated Defenders of the Hearth and Home. Even in Germany, where already in 1880 the play had immense vogue, the theatre-going public would not put up with the "revolting" conclusion. The bewilderment of audiences had to be allayed by the attenuation and dispersion of the tragic theme. Ibsen himself finally preferred to furnish a happy ending rather than leave the makeshift to the clumsy hands of hired mechanics. . . .

The charge that Ibsen wrote *A Doll's House* as an attempt not to reform but to break up the institution of marriage is too utterly ridiculous for refutation. And the virtuous disgust with the course of the action, in particular with Nora for wantonly breaking the holiest of home ties to gratify a sublimated species of selfishness, strongly recalls the impression produced by *Antony and Cleopatra* on a British matron, who regretfully referred to the conduct of Shakespeare's heroine as "so different from the home life of our own dear Queen." It goes without saying that Ibsen believed in the institution. But he was not primarily interested in institutions but in human beings. Without any conscious design, as we have seen, he was drawn into the woman movement. To him more than to any other individual factor the gradual crystallizing of public opinion on its issues is due. In the seventies of the past century he was already in advance of the position so faintheartedly taken now by the average ladylike male champion of woman's rights. Instead of dallying with the old debating-club questions, Shall woman study?—vote?—practice a profession?—Ibsen hoists into the light the main consideration, Shall woman truly live? To live, in Ibsen's sense, is to be an individual. And individuality requires freedom. His natural dislike for womankind is at once overwhelmed by his entire moral and mental clarity.

Most men, of course, would deny that women are unfree or unhappy in their lot. In the words of Mr. Bernard Shaw, they have come to think that the nursery and the kitchen are the natural sphere of a woman, exactly as English children come to think that a cage is the natural sphere of a parrot. But if men are sincere in their desire that love of the higher personal liberty be wrought into the fibre of the nation, so that, in Walt Whitman's phrase, the world may be peopled by "a larger, saner brood"; if they have faith in the recipe, "Produce great persons, the rest follows,"—then how, in the name of common sense, can they perpetuate their squatter's claim to the exclusive right of personality? Ibsen believes with John Stuart Mill in extending that right to women. But if, then, you grant to woman the status of personality, you must not restrain her from its exercise. Ibsen's working thesis, so to speak, is this: a person's responsibility to herself should prevail over other responsibilities with which it may come into collision. Evidently, then, the woman question is closely bound up with the marriage question, and in fact Ibsen's dramas deal with the conjugal fates of women, not with their virginal romances.

According to Ibsen's social code, matrimony should not be the end of freedom. That is no true family where the husband counts for everything and the wife for nothing. Children reared in such a home are very apt to develop into tyrants if boys, and, if girls, into drudges or—dolls.

WHEN DOLLS AWAKEN

The acquiescence of the average woman of the upper classes in her exclusion from her husband's intellectual interests, her felicity in material comforts, and her childish enjoyment of the banalities that crowd her days, indicate, so it would seem, a spiritual kinship with the pampered, frivolous, and, so far as she knows, completely happy mistress of the Doll's House. Will she also, sooner or later, rise in revolt and strike out for freedom—freedom at whatever cost?

For note that Nora Helmer in Ibsen's drama, the "squirrel," the "butterfly," who has never had any opinions of her own, determines of a sudden to think and act for herself:—

> Henceforth I can't be satisfied with what most people say, and what is in books. I must think things out for myself, and try to get clear about them.

Her tragic awakening to her actual position is precipitated by her discovery of her husband's inability to identify himself with her romantic conception of his character. Recollect that she had committed a punishable act, though in ignorance of the law, in order to save the life of her husband who had to be taken away to rebuild his shattered health. He being without means, it was a case of borrow or die, but Nora realized that

Helmet would rather face death than debt, so the money, obtained from a lender, must appear as a gift from Nora's father, then lying at death's door. The lender insists on the father's indorsement, for better security. The sick man, however, must not be worried with such a transaction, so Nora lightheartedly attaches his signature to the paper, as a matter of course. After that all things go exceedingly well with the Helmers till Nora of a sudden is threatened with exposure. Krogstad, the holder of the forged note, has been discharged from his modest position in the bank of which Helmer has just been appointed director, and he uses his power over Nora to extort her intercession with her husband. Nora, to whom her deed now appears in the light of its possible consequences, is in despair, because she never doubts for a moment what Helmer will do when the secret comes out: to save her honor, he will speak a heroic lie, shoulder the guilt himself, and thus wreck his brilliant career. Too little is apt to be made of this very important point by actresses and audiences. It suffices by itself to explain Nora's sudden revulsion of feeling when under the even polish of his virtues this pattern of masculine righteousness comes forth in his rank egoism. After the truth is revealed, and Nora is about to leave Helmer, he demands to know:—

> And can you also make clear to me how I have forfeited your love?
>
> NORA. Yes, I can. It was this evening, when the miracle did not happen; for then I saw you were not the man I had imagined.

Helmer's chief concern, on learning the distressing truth, is with the danger of his situation. The fear of social and even legal penalty makes him behave as a coward; he is ready to hush the matter up on the blackmailer's own conditions. To the motives of Nora's act her idolized champion is utterly blind and requites that proof of self-effacing love with resentful condemnation. Thus her affection suddenly loses its object; Helmer becomes like a stranger to her. Nora is right in feeling that it would require the miracle of miracles to change both their natures so that after this their living together should be a marriage. Helmer's shallow-souled hope at the last moment, that this miracle of miracles will happen, is vain. Nora must leave her husband . . . because living nominally as wife with a man who is either too far above or too far below her in character and intellect is, for a self-respecting woman, suggestive of moral and physical bondage.

Ibsen and the Language of Women

Inga-Stina Ewbank

Professor Emerita of English Literature at the University of Leeds in England and translator of Ibsen's *Pillars of the Community* for John Barton's Royal Shakespeare Company production in 1977, Inga-Stina Ewbank writes that Ibsen's Nora provides proof that women have to be "bilingual in a male society." Indeed, Nora alters her language depending on with whom she is speaking. To Torvald, her language is that of "female helplessness"; to Dr. Rank, she is flirtatious; and even to Mrs. Linde, she initially speaks in tones "governed by what a clever little wife should sound like."

Ibsen was not a sociolinguist—he would have scorned the term, had it existed in his day—but the terms and findings of sociolinguists *may* help us to understand his art. And, conversely, his art may do more than scientific research can, to reveal to us whether there is such a thing as woman's language and, if so, when and why and how it is spoken. . . .

His plays are not meant to be slavish imitations of life, couched in a language such as men, and women, do use, but imaginative projections of his vision of life—making contact, of course, with their audience and readers by their likeness to life such as we know it, but not stopping there. Similarly, his language, while like enough to what we hear around us to make us feel that we are listening to 'real' men and women, is primarily in the service of his vision—part of works written in prose, but with the imaginative coherence of poems.

Relatedly, the social issues which his prose plays often raise—and in particular those written in the late seventies and early eighties—are not there for their own propagandist value but as part of a larger vision of life. It is well known

Excerpted from Inga-Stina Ewbank, "Ibsen and the Language of Women," in *Women Writing and Writing About Women*, edited by Mary Jacobus (London: Croom Helm, 1979). Reprinted by permission of the author and publisher.

that, when the Norwegian Society for Women's Rights in 1898 gave a banquet for Ibsen, the aged playwright disconcerted his hostesses by making a speech in which he disclaimed any connection with women's rights. 'Of course,' he said, 'it is incidentally desirable to solve the problem of women; but that has not been my whole object. My task has been the portrayal of human beings.' Obviously his statement contains a false dichotomy: the problem of women *versus* the portrayal of human beings. And of course he knew it. He was not betraying the insights of *A Doll's House* and the other twenty-three plays he had written but was teaching his listeners the lesson that the portrayal of women is not a separate issue from the portrayal of human beings generally; and that, if you portray human beings with the sensitivity of a poet, then you are, if not solving, at least exploring the problem of women. . . .

In the play which followed *Pillars of the Community, The Doll's House,* the language of both men and women is still largely tied to the exploration of a social theme. Not that the play stands or falls on Women's Rights; in the role-playing relationship of Nora and Thorvald Helmer there are insights into the gap between woman and man, the failure of communication between husband and wife, which are quite timeless—or, as some would prefer to put it, surprisingly modern. But the language which is given to Nora is clearly meant to outline for us the curve of her development, from being Thorvald's plaything to discovering that she must leave her doll's house and go out to find herself. Until her moment of recognition, it is made very clear that man enforces on woman a type of behaviour *and* a language to go with it. Nora speaks with the 'female helplessness' which Thorvald expects of her, when she speaks to *him:* she has a different idiom when she speaks to Mrs Linde, though this is still governed by her notion of what a clever little wife should sound like, just as her flirtation with the dismal Dr Rank seems very much made up to an expected pattern; only in the odd moments of lonely agony, when the suicide decision looms, does she seem to have anything of a voice of her own. But she can switch from this to the language Thorvald expects, at the drop of a hat, or the appearance of a husband; as at the end of Act II:

> NORA (*stands for a moment as though to collect herself, then looks at her watch*). Five. Seven hours to midnight. Then

twenty-four hours to the next midnight. Then the tarantella will be over. Twenty-four and seven? Thirty-one
hours to live.

HELMER (*in the doorway, right*). What's happened to our little skylark?

NORA (*running towards him with open arms*). Here she is!

Nora is a living—or, as Ibsen would have said, a *'digtet'*—
proof of the point maintained by many modern sociolinguists: that women have to be bilingual in a male society. Indeed she has several languages. In the last scene, when she
is facing her husband after her recognition and resolution,
she yet again speaks a different one: restrained, simple, but
logically connected statements. I think Ibsen may be trying
to do what Wesker did with Beattie Bryant at the end of
Roots—to show a woman finding her own, new language.
Dramatically, I doubt if he is even as successful as Wesker;
in recent productions, at least, I have found this scene af-
fecting me more with the inadequacy of Helmer's language
to deal with the situation than with any really *felt* sense of
discovery in Nora. But then this might have been exactly Ibsen's intention—not to underline a thesis but, in his own
words, 'to portray human beings' (of either sex).

It is perhaps a pity that it was Nora who first created 'Ibsenism' in this country and who came to connect the name
of Ibsen with the idea of the new, liberated woman. The first
performance of an unexpurgated Ibsen play was that of *A
Doll's House* (with Janet Achurch as Nora) at the Novelty
Theatre on 7 June 1889 and it brought him overnight fame
and notoriety. As the editor of *Ibsen: The Critical Heritage*
points out, 'for years—in some quarters even today—it was
impossible to discuss Ibsen without referring to the position
of women in society.'. . .

Statistical surveys conducted by contemporary re-
searchers into linguistic sex differences seem ironically, for
all the desire not to fall back on stereotyped notions of sex
roles, to have found a set of predictable characteristics ap-
plying to female as against male language: it is simpler, using shorter sentences and fewer subclauses; and this also involves it being, in construction and syntax, more illogical
and incoherent. It is also more emotional; and, finally, it is
more adapted to the situation in which the speech occurs
than its male counterpart. It is a curious fact that these characteristics could also be said to describe the style of Ibsen, as

against the standard literary Norwegian of his day. . . . If I have to draw a conclusion at all, it is that Ibsen came to see the predicament of modern man (in the sense of 'human being') as most acutely realised in the predicament of modern woman; and that, to write his plays about human beings, he needed the emotional quality, the inconsequentiality, the staccato of simple sentences, the sense that experience is constantly outstripping both the vocabulary and the structure of language, which he found in the language of women. But conclusions are precarious when we deal with Ibsen whose favourite retort was 'On the contrary!'—and who would have been the first to point to one ineluctable but logically devastating flaw in this paper; that it is composed in woman's language.

Truth and Freedom in *A Doll's House*

Henry Rose

Author of *Maeterlinck's Symbolism: The Blue Bird* and other critical works, Henry Rose explores issues of truth and freedom in *A Doll's House*. Rose notes Ibsen's belief that women's status in education and marriage led to a denial of true freedom at home and in society. Such denial, as seen in *A Doll's House*, leads women to deceit and "artfulness." Nora's own thoughts of freedom cause her not only to make a habit of lying to her husband but also to break the law. It is her lack of moral perception that is ultimately to blame for her actions, Rose states. Had Nora had proper education and the same freedoms as men, her family tragedy would not have occurred.

If the spirits of Truth and Freedom are the Pillars of Society, it is in the relations of men and women, especially as represented in marriage and in the life of the family, that they first must be established. In nothing is it more necessary that Truth and Freedom should prevail than in those relations. It may be assumed from the treatment of the character of Lona in "Pillars of Society" that woman's claim to economic and social independence, and in general to more full development and a greater exercise of power in the practical affairs of life, was one of the many problems now engaging Ibsen's attention. "It is you women," exclaims Bernick at the end of the play, "who are the pillars of society," for he feels that it is by woman's influence that he has been redeemed. But Lona, a noble pioneer of her sex, replies to him in the words upon which I have commented already: "The spirits of Truth and Freedom—these are the Pillars of Society." It was on the assertion of these qualities that Lona's influence had depended. But Ibsen well knew that he had drawn a wholly exceptional type of woman when he

Excerpted from Henry Rose, *Henrik Ibsen: Poet, Mystic, and Moralist* (New York: Haskell House, 1973). Reprinted by permission of the publisher.

drew Lona. What were the conditions that led to this type being so rare? Brooding long and earnestly upon this question,
Ibsen next wrote "A Doll's House."

I regard it as evidence of the transcendent genius of Ibsen
that when he applied himself to the task of writing his next
play he chose a character like Nora as the central figure. His
problem was to illustrate the cramping effects on woman's
development of the prevalent ideas on the subject of marriage,
the paramount necessity for Truth and Freedom in this most
sacred relationship, and the pre-eminent right of woman to
the fullest development of her individuality. An inferior
dramatist, purposing to treat such a theme as this, would have
given us as the central figure of his play a robust, self-poised
woman, like Lona in "Pillars of Society," or one with all the
moral qualities of a Griselda [the medieval romance charac-
ter] united to the daring of a Joan of Arc. And this woman,
who no doubt would have been regarded as a heroine by the
whole of her sex, would have been represented as mated to a
husband who not only misunderstood her virtues, but had in
himself most of the vices of the brute. . . .

But Ibsen's truth to Nature and his fine sense of psychology
forbade a course such as this. He saw that the prevalent ideas
on the education of women and on marriage, involved the
practical denial of freedom, and that in many cases much of
the homage which men paid to women was insincere and selfish—insincere in so far as it cloaked contempt for an intellect
which men in general felt to be inferior to their own, and selfish in so far as its object was the better to secure the companionship of the woman as a glorified plaything. In Ibsen's view
there could be no reality in marriage under these conditions.
Denial of freedom, insincerity and selfishness on the one side
provoked corresponding vices on the other. The practice of the
deceit which we politely call "artfulness" was almost universal
amongst women, and petty lying and chicanery were—well,
not rare. Moreover, whilst the predisposition of nearly all
women was towards purity, in the restricted and false relationships in which they commonly stood towards men they
had acquired a preternatural sense of the power which their
sexual attraction enabled them to exercise.

Nora's Thoughts of Freedom

These were the factors of the situation which Ibsen had before him when he drew Nora. Reared as a doll-child by her

father, she had been treated as a doll-wife by her husband, who, on his part, was a quite estimable middle-class citizen. We may dismiss the more sexual aspect of the picture which Ibsen presents by observing merely that in Nora we have a woman who respects her vows of marriage to the full, but well knows the secrets of her power over her husband. To him she is indeed sincerely attached. For the sake of gaining the greater influence over him she has become a liar by habit. Fibs drop from her lips with the utmost facility, and concealment and prevarication are common features of her conduct. But her gravest delinquency of all—and it is on this that the plot of the play turns—has been an act of forgery for the purpose of raising money, partly to gratify her pride and extravagance, and partly to enable her husband to have a long holiday at the outset of their married life, a holiday on which she persuades herself that his health depends.

The details of the plot do not here concern me. But I would like to point out that it seems to me requisite to the understanding of this play as a natural and true picture of a woman's revolt, that we should perceive that the climax which is reached in the final act, when the forgery is made known to Helmer, the husband—when he and Nora come into an acute conflict, and Nora quits his roof, with the descent of the curtain whilst we hear the slamming of the outer door—does not in reality mark the period when Nora first conceives the idea of taking her own course, and of asserting her right to individuality and freedom. We may reasonably infer that Nora has been revolving this idea in her mind before ever the curtain rose even on Act I of the play; it is probable that when we see her in the earlier scenes her mind is already almost made up.

Of the fact that it is present to her thought that the need to quit her husband's roof may arise there is actual evidence in the second act. At the beginning of this act she remarks to the nurse Anna that she cannot have her children so much with her in future. The nurse consolingly answers, "Well, little children get used to anything." In response Nora says, "Do you think so? Do you believe that they would forget their mother if she went quite away?"

It is just because the treatment which she has all along received has made her, like most members of her sex, a clever actress in real life, that her growing purpose has been so well concealed. Of the moral delinquency of the forgery she is scarcely sensible, owing partly to the limitations of her training, and partly to her belief that purely generous motives had impelled her to the commission of this offence. But she is dimly conscious that her husband, on his part, may take a serious view of her conduct. If, taking that view, he yet should be ready to sacrifice himself on her behalf, though she would not accept such a sacrifice, she would regard the offer of it as proof of his real nobility, and strive to work out her redemption under his roof. But this, to use her own term, is a "miracle" for which she scarcely hopes.

NORA'S LACK OF MORAL PERCEPTION

That Nora should have conceived it as, at any rate, possible that her husband would seriously contemplate, or even offer to take on himself the responsibility for a crime of which he was all along innocent, and of which he was ignorant until he learned the truth, not from Nora, but, in despite of Nora, from a man whom he had reason to detest, indicates that her moral perceptions and her reasoning powers alike were very greatly at fault. It is not the purpose of the author that we should think them otherwise. We are not even to suppose that in the manner in which, finally, she seeks to solve her difficulties, he is holding her up for our admiration.

It is one consequence of the wrong training of women as a class that in numerous cases their moral perceptions and power of judgment, and their power to act with wisdom in great crises are partly destroyed or remain undeveloped. Nora, in this play, acts precisely as a woman of her type would act in like circumstances. If the event should prove that she was wrong in the decision which she came to and on which she acted, if it should be found that real harm was done by it to her husband and children, and that she herself even missed the goal after which she was striving—well, all these things are part of the price which Society is paying for its blunders. . . .

Ibsen did not give us a play containing a sequel to "A Doll's House." But he did give us other plays from which we may infer that whatever form the sequel would have taken, it would not have given support to the view that problems such as are presented in "A Doll's House" can be solved by the breaking of contracts, the evasion of obligations, the cutting of knots, or any expedients of that kind.

A Woman Appreciates Ibsen

Katharine M. Rogers

Professor Emerita of English at Brooklyn College,
Katharine M. Rogers appreciates Ibsen's work for its
efforts to confront the psychological means by which
women are stereotyped by society. Rogers claims that
while many critics ignore or devalue the feminism of
his plays, Ibsen's work clearly suggests an underlying
empathy for women. Finally, Rogers rejects critics'
tendency to read *A Doll's House* as a treatise for *human* rights, a reading which denies the play's message about women's rights. Such critics, she says,
need to "confront the uncomfortable realities" in their
own or "society's attitude toward women."

Women who see *A Doll's House* are stirred not only by its theatrical effectiveness, but by something rarer—a heightened
awareness of the conditions in which they live. What the play
brings home to them is that, though men no longer address
their wives as skylarks, Torvald Helmer's belittlement covered by affection remains characteristic of the male's attitude
toward the female in America [during the 1970s]. Surface conditions have changed, but the essence of the relationship, for
most couples, remains disturbingly like what Ibsen depicted
one hundred years ago.

For example, as long as most wives remain economically
dependent on their husbands, Ibsen's revelation of the connection between this dependency and a subject status remains relevant. Earning power tends to equal worth in bourgeois society, and the knowledge that one's work is worth
money does increase respect in others' eyes and even in one's
own. This point is brought out in the play by Nora's wish for
money for Christmas (money represents freedom, because it
can be spent on goods or pleasures, or saved, or used to free

Excerpted from Katharine M. Rogers, "A Woman Appreciates Ibsen," *The Centennial
Review*, Spring 1974. Reprinted by permission of the author and publisher. Notes in the
original have been omitted in this reprint.

oneself from financial worry) and Torvald's denying her this independent choice, by Nora's enjoyment of the copying work she did at night, despite her fatigue ("earning money like that. It was almost like being a man.") and the necessity of keeping it a secret from Torvald.

Again, Ibsen recognized the subtle psychological means by which society conditions women to confirm the belittling stereotype which men make of them. While he frankly dramatized Nora's callousness about "strangers," her habitual use of irrational means to persuade her husband, her dependence on his judgment, her faked ignorance of the method by which syphilis is transmitted, Ibsen made clear that these are not personal weaknesses in Nora nor biological ones in her sex, but rather the products of society's brainwashing. People with limited education and experience naturally have sympathies confined to their domestic circle and find it difficult to comprehend abstract issues; people without authority resort to lies and tricks to gain their ends; people indoctrinated to respect male judgment accept it without question; people treated like children act like children.

Ibsen could never have achieved so penetrating an analysis of the male-female relationship if he had not had extraordinary empathy with women. . . .

THE CRITIC'S REACTIONS

The feminism which Ibsen developed in *A Doll's House* and *Ghosts*, he introduced into every one of the plays of his maturity. . . . This surely proves that Ibsen had an unusually enlightened attitude toward women and was seriously concerned with women's rights rather than merely using them as a timely theme for *A Doll's House*. Nevertheless, most critical authorities either ignore Ibsen's feminism or take pains to explain it away. . . . They disparage *A Doll's House* . . . which sympathetically represents women striving to throw off male tutelage; . . . they sneer at Nora . . . who shows a constructive potential to remake [herself] and social institutions. It is the idea that *good* women could be striving for self-realization that is so hard to accept.

The only critics who recognize Ibsen's feminism and appreciate its dramatization in *A Doll's House* . . . appear to be Bernard Shaw (whose interpretation of Ibsen is usually dismissed as totally wrong-headed), Brian Downs, F.L. Lucas, John Northam, and Eva Le Gallienne. Some critics condemn

Nora, . . . though on slightly more sophisticated grounds than the Victorians did; and others disparage *A Doll's House* . . . as unworthy of [its] author—technically incompetent, outdated, or tiresomely didactic. Those who admire the play deny, explicitly or implicitly that [it has] anything to do with women's rights. . . .

[One] subtle method of devaluing the message of *A Doll's House* is to attack the play on artistic grounds. Most often these attacks focus on the ending. Thus Robert Brustein declares that "a long discussion follows after the play has, for all intents and purposes, concluded"—in spite of the fact that Ibsen himself wrote that "it was for the sake of the last scene that the whole play was written." It is amazing how often critics revive the error that the alternative "happy ending" which Ibsen wrote for the play, which he produced under duress and invariably called a "barbarous outrage," betrays uncertainty on his part about how his play should end.

Other critics declare that *A Doll's House* fails because Ibsen was too intent on preaching his message, or that the play is so old-fashioned in dramaturgy or ideas that it no longer need be taken seriously. Walter Kerr, reviewing the most recent New York production, gleefully reckoned up the play's improbabilities, such as Nora's miraculous maturation between Acts II and III, and concluded that "we must struggle to induce in ourselves a state of mind that holds humor at bay in honor of the social proposition being so implausibly stated." Raymond Williams sees *A Doll's House* as a mere variation on stock romantic melodrama, except for the final discussion, which is a declaration by Nora rather than a dramatic "confrontation between actual people." For a truly original presentation of male-female relationships we must look to [playwright August] Strindberg's *The Father*, which of course happens to be intensely misogynistic.

The play's ideas can be neutralized by oversimplification to the point that they need not disturb the complacency of any moderately liberal person, as when H.L. Mencken declared that *A Doll's House* merely says "that it is unpleasant and degrading for a wife to be treated as a mere mistress and emptyhead." Confident that Nora's battle has long been won, John George Robertson claims that "Only very young souls are still thrilled" by her slamming the door, and M.C. Bradbrook finds Nora's situation "sixty-five years behind the times" and her "sense of 'duty towards myself'" primitive.

Such interpretations soon break down if one pays close attention to what Ibsen is saying about male oppression of the female. Patronage and belittlement need not be so heavy-handed as Torvald's, and the vote and higher education have not radically changed woman's position of domestic helpmate. One wonders how many of those who glibly agree with Ibsen's ideas would in practice endorse Nora's declaration that she has a "sacred" duty to herself, that she is "first and foremost" not a wife and mother, but "an individual, just as much as" a man is.

Those who do acknowledge the greatness of *A Doll's House* often evade its implications by denying that it really deals with male-female relationships in marriage. While Ibsen dramatized "the woman's revolt against the tyrannizing male" in *A Doll's House,* Brustein declares, "and Strindberg, the male's revolt against the tyrannical woman" in *The Father,* only Strindberg really cared about the "woman question": "Ibsen was completely indifferent to it except as a metaphor for individual freedom. Nora's real antagonist is not Torvald, but society itself, insofar as it restricts her desire . . . for self-realization." It is significant that Brustein finds that only the misogynistic author meant what he said about women; he also considers Strindberg's play more powerful.

[Robert M.] Adams agrees that the "real theme" of *A Doll's House* "has nothing to do with the sexes"; it deals with a personal conflict and proposes no generalizations about men and women. Michael Meyer assures us that "*A Doll's House* is no more about women's rights than Shakespeare's *Richard II* is about the divine right of kings." While he rightly defines Ibsen's theme as "the need of every individual to find out the kind of person he or she really is and to strive to become that person," he ignores Ibsen's evidence that in our society this enterprise is far more difficult for women than for men. Though *A Doll's House* does deal with "woman's place in a man's world," Eric Bentley admits, it is more significantly concerned with "the tyranny of one human being over another; in this respect the play would be just as valid were Torvald the wife and Nora the husband." (Imagine Nora calling Torvald her little skylark.)

There is no question that Ibsen's overriding concern, throughout his works, was with the freedom and self-realization of the individual. But it is equally clear that in *A Doll's House* he was concerned specifically with that of the female individual. The forces which cramp Nora are the ignorance of life and general principles, the dependence on her husband, the narrow view of herself which a patriarchal society imposes on women. Torvald's blindness to Nora's feelings, as when he persists in making love to her in the last scene, his fury when she finds in him the supposedly feminine weakness of pettiness, his delight in twitting her over the supposed ineffectuality of her efforts to create even Christmas decorations are examples, specifically, of men's treatment of women. Torvald's belittlement clothed with affection and his assumption that he monopolizes the judgment and strength in the household are characteristic of husbands, not wives. Torvald perfectly illustrates, as so many husbands still do, the truth of a statement by Ibsen's contemporary John Stuart Mill: "the generality of the male sex cannot yet tolerate the idea of living with an equal." Of course society limits men too—as Ibsen dramatized in many of his plays—but that is not his concern here.

WOMEN'S RIGHTS, HUMAN RIGHTS

Those who deny that Ibsen was particularly sympathetic to women and their struggle for freedom triumphantly cite statements in which he explicitly disclaimed being a feminist. They may even dismiss unmistakable cases, such as his support for a bill to assure married women control of their own property, as strange aberrations from his usual attitude. Actually, Ibsen's sympathy with women's rights is evidenced not only by his support for this bill but by his impassioned efforts toward giving women equal membership privileges in the Scandinavian Society in Rome and by numerous statements in his letters.

Ibsen wanted something more significant than votes for women: political influence. He thought that women, not men, should have been consulted about the married women's property bill ("To consult men on such a matter is like asking wolves if they desire better protection for the sheep"). He would have liked to see "all the unprivileged," including of course women, form a truly strong, progressive party to press for such goals as "the statutory improvement of the position of woman" and educational reform. Surely Ibsen would have been pleased to see the formation of the National Women's Political Caucus in [America].

Ibsen's moderate involvement in women's rights issues is doubly remarkable in view of his resistance to any party identification and his scepticism about institutional reforms. It was crucially important to him to be an individual always, never tied to any group or party program; and he was convinced that outward freedoms, such as the right to vote, meant little in comparison to that inward freedom from ignorance, bigotry, convention, or blind belief in authority which he constantly campaigned for both in men and women. What point would there have been in giving the vote to a Nora who worshipped Torvald? Once free psychologically, Nora can be a human being regardless of legal or political restrictions.

Critics like to quote Ibsen's most explicit statement on feminism—his Speech at the Banquet of the Norwegian League for Women's Rights, 1898—to prove that he had no interest in female emancipation. While this speech must indeed have chilled the suffragists at the banquet, its apparent hostility results from Ibsen's aversion to party affiliation of any kind and his resentment at being reduced to a mere polemicist, a preacher of specific political programs rather than an artist. Hence he announced that he never wrote with "any conscious thought of making propaganda," never "consciously worked for the women's rights movement," was "not even quite clear as to just what this women's rights movement really is." But, having disposed of the easy oversimplifications, Ibsen went on to make clear that his real purpose was actually what the women were campaigning for, seen from a broader perspective, since rights for women are "a problem of mankind in general." Ibsen fought for human rights rather than specifically for women's rights—but, unlike so many libertarians, never forgot that the first include the second.

Though Ibsen declared in this speech that women could contribute best to society as mothers, he was not trying to reduce them to helpmates to men. He specifically said "mothers"—not wives and mothers, as he is sometimes misquoted—and thereby focused on the function which is of primary importance to women and which demands independent creative effort. His exhortation to women to "solve the human problem. As mothers," the only capacity in which they can solve it, should not be taken as a hypocritical persuasion to subservience in the manner of Dickens or John Ruskin. Ibsen did not think of mothers as mere nursemaids, but wanted them to improve future generations by developing culture and discipline in their children—something only strong, enlightened people can achieve.

Ibsen's original notes for ... *A Doll's House* support this interpretation. ... Considering Nora's childishness, Ibsen deplored the state of mothers in contemporary society, who might as well go away and die, like insects, once they have completed the work of physical propagation. Since a woman cannot be a good mother without being an adequate human being, loving little Nora, who delights in petting and playing with her children, rightly tells Torvald that she is not qualified to bring them up. Feminists today naturally think in terms of professions or political office, but the essential point remains, as Ibsen recognized, the emancipation of the mind.

Ibsen's sympathy with women did not show itself as a doctrinaire obsession with such things as woman suffrage or equal job opportunities. It followed from his concern for human rights—but I reiterate that only a man of Ibsen's exceptional honesty and enlightenment would have recognized that it followed. His particular interest in women probably stemmed from his observation that they were more subject to traditional authority than men, while less attached to conventional thinking because they had less vested interest in the Establishment. Thus they were both more victimized by the social restrictions on free development and more openminded to spiritual revolution.

It might at first seem paradoxical that this defender of women was so markedly disenchanted with romantic love: far from glorifying his ideal, Ibsen made a point of discrediting it . . . in *A Doll's House,* where the male oppressor is outwardly a good husband and very much in love with the wife he disparages and exploits. Actually, this disenchantment may have clarified his awareness of women's oppression. He probably recognized that romantic idealization of women has all too often been used to stifle their right to self-realization. Idealization of the "good" lover or wife is an effective way to reconcile men's exploitation and patronage of women with their reluctance to admit hostility. To strip away this idealization in order to show good women striving for an independent existence is deeply threatening, for it both undermines men's privileged position and prevents them from cloaking it under professions of love and admiration for women.

Nora . . . [is] unacceptable to many readers because [her] striving to be independent is presented as justified. The traditional male attitude is that women should exist to fulfill men's needs—to be objects of romantic fantasy, or supporters of the masculine ego, or self-immolating servants, or eager appreciators of male sexual prowess. Although female roles may change . . . the attitude remains that a good woman does not what she wants to do but what some man wants her to do.

Yet, because Ibsen is recognized as a major author of contemporary significance, his ideas cannot be dismissed out of hand. They must somehow be reconciled to the sensibilities of readers who find Strindberg's misogyny more "true" than Ibsen's insistence that women are entitled to the same independent self-realization that men are. While some critics solve the difficulty by asserting that . . . *A Doll's House* [is] inferior to Ibsen's other, "more characteristic" work, others are forced to many ingenious readings.

Sometimes they simply denigrate the heroine, implying that Ibsen did so too: Nora is selfish, irresponsible, and unreasonable. . . .

Rarely do the critics recognize that Ibsen represented Nora . . . as shackled by social influences. In general, they deal with his presentation of these pressures by ignoring it or reducing it to inconsequence. . . . In the case of *A Doll's House,* Ibsen's advocacy of women's rights is often dismissed by the old technique of ridicule: Ibsen himself did not take them seriously, and represented Nora as a comic victim of self-delusion; or, if in earnest, he unwittingly made his theme ridiculous by resorting to clumsy dramatic technique or limiting himself to a cause dated and irrelevant in the emancipated state of present society.

Those who feel compelled to react seriously to Nora and *A Doll's House* reconcile their admiration with their reluctance to think about women's rights by claiming that the play is about human rights in general. Such an interpretation frees the critic from any need to re-evaluate his conventional assumptions, to confront uncomfortable realities in his own or society's attitude toward women.

CHAPTER 4

Major Themes

READINGS ON
A DOLL'S HOUSE

Money, Survival, and Independence in *A Doll's House*

Bernard F. Dukore

Author and Ibsen scholar Bernard F. Dukore writes that money is such an integral part of the atmosphere of Nora's household that it is fitting that questions of personal independence should arise from it. Indebtedness is another key theme in the play, and as financial dependencies shift between the acts, so do issues of emotional dependency. Unclear as to her future financial security at the end of the play, it is an emotional independence that Nora eventually reaps as she rejects Torvald and the house so dependent on money that the language of daily, ordinary conversations runs on bankers' terms.

While money may talk, characters in plays do not always talk about money. Those in Ibsenite . . . drama do—notably, in *A Doll House* . . . —for money is a major factor in the society [this] play reflects and criticizes. The absence of money means inability to survive. In the case of Torvald Helmer, lack of money—some years before the start of *A Doll House*—meant nonsurvival in the most literal sense of the term: he might have died. To acquire money, people could borrow, as his wife did, [but] . . . while the acquisition of money may enable one to survive, money does not necessarily make one independent, no matter how large the amount, for independence is a more complex matter. . . .

In *A Doll House,* money is part of the atmosphere of that house. Its need and its permeation in society create the conflicts that inform the play. It sustains or fails to sustain the home, a societal institution suggested by the title. Dependence upon money creates questions about independence

Excerpted from Bernard F. Dukore, *Money and Politics in Ibsen, Shaw, and Brecht,* by permission of the University of Missouri Press. Copyright © 1980 by the Curators of the University of Missouri. Notes in the original have been omitted in this reprint.

from it as well as from individuals and social conceptions of which it is a part. . . .

At the start of Ibsen's play, Nora Helmer enters the titular doll house; at the end, she leaves it. Between start and finish, entry and departure, Ibsen dramatizes the nature of that house, which by extension represents middle-class society. Among the foundations of this house and of middle-class society is money. But while survival is at stake, so is independence. Nevertheless, the relationship between independence and money does not form a simple one-to-one equation. Financial independence helps create individual, emotional independence, since without it, dependence and insecurity are likely to result. Yet, financial security is neither a necessary nor a sufficient cause of such independence. In *A Doll House,* Ibsen dramatizes the complex relationships among money, survival, and independence. . . .

Perceptively, Elizabeth Hardwicke points out that "almost the first line of the play is, 'How much?'" To be exact, the question occurs at the end of the play's first, three-line speech. The heroine, Nora, addresses a delivery boy, who has just carried in a Christmas tree. Not only does Ibsen establish the subject of money at the very start, he also establishes its social function: payment for services rendered. Although the fee is fifty öre, Nora gives the boy a crown (one hundred öre) and tells him to keep the change—an action that is less frivolous than festive, in harmony with the holiday season. In this five-line scene, Ibsen suggests themes of money and financial independence.

The next scene modifies the impression of financial independence. From the adjoining room, the voice of Nora's husband, Torvald Helmer, asks whether *his* little lark and *his* little squirrel has returned. Later, he calls her beauty "mine, mine alone—completely and utterly." Belonging means dependence, not independence. But if Helmer considers Nora his property, as he apparently does, Nora encourages him to do so. To him, she calls herself *his* little squirrel and *his* lark. When she pleads, "I can't get anywhere without your help. . . . Yes, take care of me, Torvald, please!" he responds in kind: "Gladly, if it's what you want." Do both desire the type of relationship in which she is dependent upon him? So it would seem.

Nora's early response to her husband returns the subject to money, and the dialogue that follows relates money to the question of independence. She invites him to see what she has bought. "Can't be disturbed," he immediately responds, a set-up for his comic entrance: "(*After a moment he opens the door and peers in, pen in hand.*) Bought, you say?" Underlying the humor that derives from the stereotyped image of the flighty wife injudiciously spending money earned by her hard-working husband, who calls her purchases "throwing money around again," the scene firmly establishes the themes that the immediately preceding scene implied: money and financial independence. At the same time, it reverses the play's initial suggestion that those who dwell in this house are financially independent. In this house, matters are not necessarily what they seem to be, particularly such matters as money and independence.

As money and lack of it are among the preoccupations of the society in which they live, so are they major concerns of the Helmers. Until this Christmas, Nora reminds her husband, they have had to economize. Now that he has acquired a well-paying job, they need not skimp but can spend freely, an appropriate way to celebrate this holiday. Since he will not actually have his higher salary in hand for another three months, he argues, they should not imprudently squander money. To use a stock-exchange image, Nora is speculating on a futures commodity. Independence, in other words, has not yet arrived. No matter, suggests she, they can borrow money. A great matter, he counters, for if they were to borrow, she to spend, and he to die, she would be entirely without resources, and her person and property would be dependent upon the wills of moneylenders. Explicitly, Helmer links money, dependence, and independence: "No debts! Never borrow! Something of freedom's lost . . . from a home that's founded on borrowing and debt."

It is appropriate to observe how economically Ibsen sets up these themes of the importance of money and its relationship to other aspects of life. Primarily money, but also indebtedness, dependence, and independence, are established within the first two pages of the play.

Helmer is a decent man, not a miser. Why did he and Nora lack money for so long? Although he used to be a lawyer, he refused to take unjust cases. As a result of such principles, he failed to earn a good or steady income. Now, matters are different, for Helmer has what Nora calls "a safe, secure job" with "a huge salary and lots of commissions." She looks forward to "stacks of money and not a care in the world." To her, stacks of money will indeed result in a life that is independent of care. To emphasize the importance of money and its relationship to independence, Ibsen gives Helmer not just any job but a job as manager of a bank. Appropriate to his new position and to the play's theme, Helmer uses financial images. He says Nora earned the applause given her tarantella, and he calls her "his richest treasure." At parties, he sends her what he terms "a stolen look."

SHIFTING DEPENDENCIES

In their society, financial independence for them means dependence for others. As Nora recognizes, "everyone who works in the bank [is] dependent now on Torvald." By contrast, their former lack of money is a direct cause of Nora's present dilemma, dependence upon the wishes of a blackmailer. Because Helmer did not earn much money at law, he had to take on extra jobs which, according to Nora, occupied him morning and night, and wore him down until he fell deathly ill. His doctors declared it essential that he travel south. His health ruined by lack of money, his health could only be restored by money—4,800 crowns, the cost of the trip. Then, independence was not even an issue; survival was, and its price was money. To raise it, Nora acted independently. Forging her father's name on a promissory note, she borrowed the sum. Paradoxically, while Nora had depended for her money on Helmer's wages from his jobs, the cure for his ill health that was a consequence of those jobs depended on her independent acquisition of money. Paradoxically too, while her ability to repay the debt is dependent upon Helmer's salary, the consequences of this better-paying job—firing one of the bank workers now dependent on Helmer, Krogstad, who had lent Nora the money—make her, and, therefore, her husband, dependent on the man who is apparently dependent on Helmer.

The matters of money, survival, dependence, and independence become more complex. As these money-related paradoxes suggest, both Nora and Helmer are in different ways dependent upon each other. While Helmer treats Nora as a doll, she treats him as a doll. As a bank manager, he manages money. Though not a bank manager, she does too. True, she lacks complete understanding of business jargon. "In the business world there's what they call quarterly interest and what they call amortization," she says, "and these are always so terribly hard to manage. . . . These accounts, you know, aren't easy to figure." Nevertheless, she has business competence. Although she found it difficult to do so, she met her payments on time. Apparently a dependent doll in a doll house, Nora is an independent businesswoman who manages her household money so as to siphon off enough to pay her debt without skimping on her husband and children. She manages her domestic economy secretly and independently of her husband, who for that reason and in that sense is a doll in the house she runs.

MONEY FOR SURVIVAL

Other characters in the play parallel Nora and Helmer. Krogstad, who lent Nora the money she needed, once committed the same crime as Nora: forgery. Like Nora, Krogstad—to whom Nora is in debt—is dependent on Helmer for money: she receives it at home, he at the bank. To Krogstad, his job means more than a salary; it means survival. Potentially, it also means a life that makes him independent of his reputation as a forger, and affords a means to achieve a higher position that will enable him to demonstrate such abilities as to supplant Helmer. The financial security and independence Helmer apparently enjoys, he plans to acquire.

With Mrs. Linde, money has always been a concern. Survival, for herself and her family, has been her goal. Because she had to support a helpless mother and two small brothers, she dropped the penniless Krogstad, whom she loved, and married the apparently well-off Linde. As she puts it, using the third person, she "sold herself." But Linde's business, which turned out to be shaky, collapsed after he died. Mrs. Linde and Nora discuss her widowhood in terms of profit and loss: "And he left you nothing?" "No." "And no children?" "No." "Nothing at all, then?" "Not even a sense of loss to feed on." To Mrs. Linde, who understands the necessity of money in order to survive, independence is not invariably reducible to monetary terms. Now independent of everyone on whom she either depended or who depended on her—husband and mother dead, brothers grown up—she finds her life empty. Armed with a job (Krogstad's old job, in fact), she needs "someone to work for," but this does not mean someone to be dependent upon her money as Nora is dependent upon Helmer's. It means someone who needs her affection and understanding as much as she needs his. "We both need each other," she tells Krogstad, who agrees. Acknowledging such need, they transcend financial conceptions of dependence. With (her) wages that will enable them to survive and give him the strength to try again for a foothold in society, their emotional interdependence and mutual love, candor, and sense of responsibility supersede the question of independence.

Ibsen provides other suggestive parallels and contrasts. As Helmer used to be, Rank is in ill health. Whereas the restoration of Helmer's health depended upon a response to the question "How much?" and the cash at hand to purchase it, the wealthy Rank cannot buy his health. Even so, in the society in which he lives—a society based on buying, selling, and borrowing—he is accustomed to discuss even health in terms of money: "These past few days I've been auditing my internal accounts. Bankrupt." Financially independent, his external accounts bear no relation to his internal accounts.

Among the lower classes, money means survival, and considerations of independence are irrelevant. To Anne-Marie, the nurse of Nora's children and the nurse of Nora when she was a child, money is necessary to survive, and that is all there is to it. When she had an illegitimate child, she gave it to strangers. Why? She had to, for she needed a job, and the position offered by Nora's parents was too good for a poverty-stricken fallen woman to pass up. Unlike Nora at the end of *A Doll House,* Anne-Marie did not abandon her child in order to fulfill herself as a free, independent human being; and she did not leave the child with its father ("That slippery fish," she calls him, "he didn't do a thing for me"). She gave her child to others because she could not afford to do anything else.

Nora's Emotional Independence

Before the famous final scene between Nora and her bank-manager husband, the Helmers' lives link survival, dependence, and independence with money. During this scene, the issue for Nora is solely independence. She begins with financial imagery appropriate to his position. They are, she says, reaching a final settlement, closing accounts. Although money figures at the start of her description of her life—"I'd lived here as a beggar"—it soon becomes apparent that it is no longer the vital issue it had been. Significantly, the only reference to money beyond the initial allusions is an aborted one, in which Helmer begins to offer her some and she interrupts him before he can speak the word aloud. Though unspoken, a view of life in financial terms underlies their discussion. More pressing than what society insists she owes her husband and children, she makes clear without using such terms, is her debt to herself. Nora insists that she learn for herself what life really is, what ethics really are. No longer should Helmer feel bound to her, or she to him. Symbolic of the end to their dependence upon each other, a trade seals their separation. In a reversal of the transaction that first bound them, each returns the other's wedding ring.

Independent of bank-manager Helmer, Nora uses language that is independent of banking terms. What of her debt to her children? In the second act, Ibsen makes clear that Anne-Marie will be present to care for them. Why does not Nora prudently put money in her purse before she leaves? In the first act, she does, forty crowns, which Helmer extracts from his wallet (a visually emphatic action) so that she may purchase something for herself, not the house, during the holiday season. This, she does—though not in the way he (or she) imagines at the time. With the money, she presumably can return to her home town to start a new life. Independent at the end of the play, free of her debt to Krogstad and of her tie to her bank-manager husband, Nora no longer speaks in images that connect her to either. To Nora, money, survival, and independence become her private, personal concerns—not those of her husband.

But Nora at the end of the play is not essentially different from Nora at the beginning. She is only different from what she seemed to be. Earlier, she managed the household finances and was skillful enough to manipulate money in order to meet her payments when they came due. Why imagine that she will be less skillful in future? At the end of the play, Nora acts not only independently but unconventionally as well. Here too, she is no different from what she was previously, when she managed to go it alone to borrow a large sum of money and to commit forgery in order to secure the loan. The presence of Anne-Marie notwithstanding, does Nora lack consideration for her children? Perhaps, though here too Nora at the end of the play is no different from the earlier Nora. "But didn't you ever consider that this [forgery] was a fraud against me?" asks Krogstad. Nora's response: "I couldn't let myself be bothered by that. You weren't any concern of mine." Then and now, when Nora establishes a priority, she considers all other values unimportant. What is different at the end of *A Doll House* is that Nora acts for herself alone. For her self-fulfillment, she requires independence.

In the middle-class society depicted by Ibsen, survival, dependence, and independence relate to money, and Ibsen dramatizes these relationships. But they are neither simple (one-to-one) nor constant. Although he links them verbally when they are organically connected to each other, he verbally dissociates them from each other when he stresses the dissociation of an exemplar of independence from the criterion of money, and from one of its exemplars. Ibsen regards individual fulfillment as primary, but its nature varies according to the individual. To Mrs. Linde and Krogstad, survival requires money, but ultimately, emotional independence demands a mutually dependent, candid, and responsible relationship between wife and husband. To Nora, plagued for years by a dependence upon money, independence demands an initial dissociation from considerations of money and from ties associated overtly and covertly with money. At the end of *A Doll House,* leaving husband and house, she achieves emotional independence.

Technical Novelty in Ibsen's Plays

George Bernard Shaw

Renowned author and socialist George Bernard
Shaw discusses Ibsen's technical novelty in his use
of the "discussion," such as in Nora's final scene
with Torvald, for example—the discussion that precedes her final exit. Despite formal criticism from reviewers who feel the discussion technique is not dramatic enough for the stage, Shaw agrees with Ibsen
that the technique can make an ordinary play an extraordinary one.

Formerly you had in what was called a well made play an
exposition in the first act, a situation in the second, an un-
ravelling in the third. Now you have exposition, situation,
and discussion; and the discussion is the test of the playwright. The critics protest in vain. They declare that discussions are not dramatic, and that art should not be didactic.
Neither the playwrights nor the public take the smallest notice of them. The discussion conquered Europe in Ibsen's
Doll's House; and now the serious playwright recognizes in
the discussion not only the main test of his highest powers,
but also the real centre of his play's interest. Sometimes he
even takes every possible step to assure the public before-
hand that his play will be fitted with that newest improvement. . . .

Now when a play is only a story of how a villain tries to
separate an honest young pair of betrothed lovers; to gain
the hand of the woman by calumny; and to ruin the man by
forgery, murder, false witness, and other commonplaces of
the Newgate Calendar, the introduction of a discussion
would clearly be ridiculous. . . .

But this sort of drama is soon exhausted by people who go
often to the theatre. In twenty visits one can see every possi-

Excerpted from "Technical Novelty in Ibsen's Plays," in *The Quintessence of Ibsenism*,
by George Bernard Shaw (London: Constable, 1926). Reprinted by permission of The
Society of Authors on behalf of the George Bernard Shaw Estate.

ble change rung on all the available plots and incidents out of which plays of this kind can be manufactured. The illusion of reality is soon lost: in fact it may be doubted whether any adult ever entertains it: it is only to very young children that the fairy queen is anything but an actress. But at the age when we cease to mistake the figures on the stage for *dramatis personæ*, and know that they are actors and actresses, the charm of the performer begins to assert itself; and the child who would have been cruelly hurt by being told that the Fairy Queen was only Miss Smith dressed up to look like one, becomes the man who goes to the theatre expressly to see Miss Smith, and is fascinated by her skill or beauty to the point of delighting in plays which would be unendurable to him without her. Thus we get plays "written round" popular performers, and popular performers who give value to otherwise useless plays by investing them with their own attractiveness. But all these enterprises are, commercially speaking, desperately precarious. To begin with, the supply of performers whose attraction is so far independent of the play that their inclusion in the cast sometimes makes the difference between success and failure, is too small to enable all our theatres, or even many of them, to depend on their actors rather than on their plays. And to finish with, no actor can make bricks entirely without straw. . . . In the long run nothing can retain the interest of the playgoer after the theatre has lost its illusion for his childhood, and its glamor for his adolescence, but a constant supply of interesting plays; and this is specially true in London, where the expense and trouble of theatregoing have been raised to a point at which it is surprising that sensible people of middle age go to the theatre at all. As a matter of fact, they mostly stay at home.

Now an interesting play cannot in the nature of things mean anything but a play in which problems of conduct and character of personal importance to the audience are raised and suggestively discussed. People have a thrifty sense of taking away something from such plays: they not only have had something for their money, but they retain that something as a permanent possession. Consequently none of the commonplaces of the box office hold good of such plays. In vain does the experienced acting manager declare that people want to be amused and not preached at in the theatre; that they will not stand long speeches; that a play must not contain more than 18,000 words; that it must not begin before nine nor last beyond eleven; that there must be no politics and no religion in it; that breach of these golden rules will drive people to the variety theatres; that there must be a woman of bad character, played by a very attractive actress, in the piece; and so on and so forth. All these counsels are valid for plays in which there is nothing to discuss. They may be disregarded by the playwright who is a moralist and a debater as well as a dramatist. From him, within the inevitable limits set by the clock and by the physical endurance of the human frame, people will stand anything as soon as they are matured enough and cultivated enough to be susceptible to the appeal of his particular form of art. The difficulty at present is that mature and cultivated people do not go to the theatre, just as they do not read penny novelets; and when an attempt is made to cater for them they do not respond to it in time, partly because they have not the habit of playgoing, and partly because it takes too long for them to find out that the new theatre is not like all the other theatres. But when they do at last find their way there, the attraction is not the firing of blank cartridges at one another by actors, nor the pretence of falling down dead that ends the stage combat, nor the simulation of erotic thrills by a pair of stage lovers, nor any of the other tomfooleries called action, but the exhibition and discussion of the character and conduct of stage figures who are made to appear real by the art of the playwright and the performers. . . .

Nora's "Discussion" Changes the Face of Theatre

Up to a certain point in the last act, A Doll's House is a play that might be turned into a very ordinary French drama by the excision of a few lines, and the substitution of a sentimental happy ending for the famous last scene: indeed the very first thing the theatrical wiseacres did with it was to effect exactly this transformation, with the result that the play thus pithed had no success and attracted no notice worth mentioning. But at just that point in the last act, the heroine very unexpectedly (by the wiseacres) stops her emotional acting and says: "We must sit down and discuss all this that has been happening between us." And it was by this new technical feature: this addition of a new movement, as musicians would say, to the dramatic form, that A Doll's House conquered Europe and founded a new school of dramatic art.

Since that time the discussion has expanded far beyond the limits of the last ten minutes of an otherwise "well made" play. The disadvantage of putting the discussion at the end was not only that it came when the audience was fatigued, but that it was necessary to see the play over again, so as to follow the earlier acts in the light of the final discussion, before it became fully intelligible. . . . Accordingly, we now have plays, including some of my own, which begin with discussion and end with action, and others in which the discussion interpenetrates the action from beginning to end. When Ibsen invaded England discussion had vanished from the stage; and women could not write plays. Within twenty years women were writing better plays than men; and these plays were passionate arguments from beginning to end. The action of such plays consists of a case to be argued. If the case is uninteresting or stale or badly conducted or obviously trumped up, the play is a bad one. If it is important and novel and convincing, or at least disturbing, the play is a good one. But anyhow the play in which there is no argument and no case no longer counts as serious drama. It may still please the child in us as [the comical puppet show] Punch and Judy does; but nobody nowadays pretends to regard the well made play as anything more than a commercial product which is not in question when modern schools of serious drama are under discussion. . . .

In the new plays, the drama arises through a conflict of unsettled ideals rather than through vulgar attachments, rapacities, generosities, resentments, ambitions, misunderstandings, oddities and so forth as to which no moral question is raised. The conflict is not between clear right and wrong: the villain is as conscientious as the hero, if not more so: in fact, the question which makes the play interesting (when it *is* interesting) is which is the villain and which the hero. Or, to put it another way, there are no villains and no heroes. This strikes the critics mainly as a departure from dramatic art; but it is really the inevitable return to nature which ends all the merely technical fashions. Now the natural is mainly the everyday; and its climaxes must be, if not everyday, at least everylife, if they are to have any importance for the spectator. Crimes, fights, big legacies, fires, shipwrecks, battles, and thunderbolts are mistakes in a play, even when they can be effectively simulated. No doubt they may acquire dramatic interest by putting a character through the test of an emergency; but the test is likely to be too obviously theatrical, because, as the playwright cannot in the nature of things have much experience of such catastrophes, he is forced to substitute a set of conventions or conjectures for the feelings they really produce.

ACCIDENTS AND CATASTROPHES

In short, pure accidents are not dramatic: they are only anecdotic. They may be sensational, impressive, provocative, ruinous, curious, or a dozen other things; but they have no specifically dramatic interest. There is no drama in being knocked down or run over. . . . Bushels of good paper have been inked in vain by writers who imagined they could produce a tragedy by killing everyone in the last act accidentally. As a matter of fact no accident, however sanguinary, can produce a moment of real drama, though a difference of opinion between husband and wife as to living in town or country might be the beginning of an appalling tragedy or a capital comedy.

It may be said that everything is an accident . . . that Torvald Helmer might just as likely have married Mrs. Nickleby as Nora. Granting this trifling for what it is worth, the fact remains that marriage is no more an accident than birth or death: that is, it is expected to happen to everybody. And if every man has a good deal of Torvald Helmer in him, and every woman a good deal of Nora, neither their characters nor their meeting and marrying are accidents. . . . Reflective people are not more interested in the Chamber of Horrors than in their own homes, nor in murderers, victims, and villains than in themselves. . . .

Perhaps the most plausible reproach levelled at Ibsen by modern critics of his own school is just that survival of the old school in him which makes the death rate so high in his last acts. Do Oswald Alving, Hedvig Ekdal, Rosmer and Rebecca, Hedda Gabler, Solness, Eyolf, Borkman, Rubeck and Irene [all characters from Ibsen's plays] die dramatically natural deaths, or are they slaughtered in the classic and Shakespearean manner, partly because the audience expects blood for its money, partly because it is difficult to make people attend seriously to anything except by startling them with some violent calamity? It is so easy to make out a case for either view that I shall not argue the point. The post-Ibsen playwrights apparently think that Ibsen's homicides and suicides were forced. . . . I myself have been reproached because the characters in my plays "talk but do nothing," meaning that they do not commit felonies. . . . If people's souls are tied up by law and public opinion it is much more tragic to leave them to wither in these bonds than to end their misery and relieve the salutary compunction of the audience by outbreaks of violence. . . .

But in Ibsen's plays the catastrophe, even when it seems forced, and when the ending of the play would be more tragic without it, is never an accident; and the play never exists for its sake. His nearest to an accident is the death of little Eyolf [the title character in *Little Eyolf*], who falls off a pier and is drowned. But this instance only reminds us that there is one good dramatic use for an accident: it can awaken people. When England wept over the deaths of little Nell and Paul Dombey [characters in Charles Dickens's *The Old Curiosity Shop* and *Dombey and Son*], the strong soul of [English writer John] Ruskin was moved to scorn: to novelists who were at a loss to make their books sell he offered the formula: When at a loss, kill a child. But Ibsen did not kill little Eyolf to manufacture pathos. The surest way to achieve a thoroughly bad performance of Little Eyolf is to conceive it as a sentimental tale of a drowned darling. Its drama lies in the awakening of Allmers and his wife to the despicable quality and detestable rancors of the life they have been idealizing as blissfull and poetic. They are so sunk in their dream that the awakening can be effected only by a violent shock. And that is just the one dramatically useful thing an accident can do. It can shock. Hence the accident that befalls Eyolf.

As to the deaths in Ibsen's last acts, they are a sweeping up of the remains of dramatically finished people.

Ibsen Gives Us "Ourselves in Our Own Situations"

The drama was born of old from the union of two desires: the desire to have a dance and the desire to hear a story. The dance became a rant: the story became a situation. When Ibsen began to make plays, the art of the dramatist had shrunk into the art of contriving a situation. And it was held that the stranger the situation, the better the play. Ibsen saw that, on the contrary, the more familiar the situation, the more interesting the play. Shakespear had put ourselves on the stage but not our situations. Our uncles seldom murder our fathers, and cannot legally marry our mothers; we do not meet witches; our kings are not as a rule stabbed and succeeded by their stabbers; and when we raise money by bills we do not promise to pay pounds of our flesh. Ibsen supplies the want left by Shakespear. He gives us not only ourselves, but ourselves in our own situations. The things that happen to his stage figures are things that happen to us. One consequence is that his plays are much more important to us than Shakespear's. Another is that they are capable both of hurting us cruelly and of filling us with excited hopes of escape from idealistic tyrannies, and with visions of intenser life in the future.

Changes in technique follow inevitably from these changes in the subject matter of the play. When a dramatic poet can give you hopes and visions, such old maxims as that stage-craft is the art of preparation become boyish, and may be left to those unfortunate playwrights who, being unable to make anything really interesting happen on the stage, have to acquire the art of continually persuading the audience that it is going to happen presently. When he can stab people to the heart by shewing them the meanness or cruelty of something they did yesterday and intend to do tomorrow, all the old tricks to catch and hold their attention become the silliest of superfluities. . . . The writer who practises the art of Ibsen therefore discards all the old tricks of preparation, catastrophe, *dénouement,* and so forth without thinking about it. . . . Ibsen substituted a terrible art of sharpshooting at the audience, trapping them, fencing with them, aiming always at the sorest spot in their consciences. Never mislead an audience, was an old rule. But the new school will trick the spectator into forming a meanly false judgment, and then convict him of it in the next act, often to his grievous mortification. When you despise something you ought to take off your hat to, or admire and imitate something you ought to loathe, you cannot resist the dramatist who knows how to touch these morbid spots in you and make you see that they are morbid. The dramatist knows that as long as he is teaching and saving his audience, he is as sure of their strained attention as a dentist is, or the Angel of the Annunciation. And though he may use all the magic of art to make you forget the pain he causes you or to enhance the joy of the hope and courage he awakens, he is never occupied in the old work of manufacturing interest and expectation with materials that have neither novelty, significance, nor relevance to the experience or prospects of the spectators.

Hence a cry has arisen that the post-Ibsen play is not a play, and that its technique, not being the technique described by Aristotle, is not a technique at all. . . . The new technique is new only on the modern stage. It has been used by preachers and orators ever since speech was invented. It is the technique of playing upon the human conscience; and it has been practised by the playwright whenever the playwright has been capable of it. Rhetoric, irony, argument, paradox, epigram, parable, the re-arrangement of haphazard facts into orderly and intelligent situations: these are both the oldest and the newest arts of the drama; and your plot construction and art of preparation are only the tricks of theatrical talent and the shifts of moral sterility, not the weapons of dramatic genius. In the theatre of Ibsen we are not flattered spectators killing an idle hour with an ingenious and amusing entertainment: we are "guilty creatures sitting at a play"; and the technique of pastime is no more applicable than at a murder trial.

The technical novelties of the Ibsen and post-Ibsen plays are, then: first, the introduction of the discussion and its development until it so overspreads and interpenetrates the action that it finally assimilates it, making play and discussion practically identical; and, second, as a consequence of making the spectators themselves the persons of the drama, and the incidents of their own lives its incidents, the disuse of the old stage tricks by which audiences had to be induced to take an interest in unreal people and improbable circumstances, and the substitution of a forensic technique of recrimination, disillusion, and penetration through ideals to the truth, with a free use of all the rhetorical and lyrical arts of the orator, the preacher, the pleader, and the rhapsodist.

Ibsen's Search for the Hero

John Northam

Professor of English at Cambridge University and
author of *Ibsen's Dramatic Method,* John Northam
explains that Ibsen's hero was that of the individual,
and the forces that this new hero had to overcome
were the pressures and limitations of society itself.
Northam refers to Nora as an example of the individual's struggle against society. He outlines her various
acts of heroism throughout the play and suggests
that it is her consistent fight and her unwillingness
to sacrifice basic principles that make her into the
play's heroine.

It is because tragedy is so invigorating, besides being dreadful and terrifying, that it is vital to the spiritual health of an
age. It suggests to us standards by which, even in the com-
monplace society which we inhabit, life can become an expression of nobility. That is why Ibsen is so vitally important
to us, for he seems to me to be the only dramatist to have
created great tragedy out of a society that can still be called
fundamentally modern. . . .

Tragedy explores the extent to which man is responsible
for his own fate. Exploration is needed, because although
man acts on the assumption that he is free to choose, he
comes into conflict with powers in the universe over which
he has no ultimate control. There is no fixed or clear de-
marcation between freedom and necessity. . . .

For Ibsen, coming when he did in time, there could be no
question but that the hero must be represented primarily as
an individual. So that one of the problems facing Ibsen, if we
can credit him with a constant ambition to write a modern
tragedy, was this: how to present on the stage a convincing
portrait of a modern individual—a man of sophisticated and

Excerpted from John Northam, "Ibsen's Search for the Hero," *Edda,* vol. 60 (Hefte 1-2,
1960). Notes in the original have been omitted in this reprint.

subtle thoughts and feelings, of modern manners and of everyday speech—and at the same time show him as possessing the full stature and grandeur of a hero.

And here we must turn to the other element in the conflict, the powers over which man has no ultimate control. For we judge a man's heroism by reference to his opponent, David in relation to Goliath. It is essential to the tragic vision that the tragic hero should be seen to be in conflict with forces that are powerfully represented.

Like the hero, the forces are differently represented in different ages. . . .

For a man of Ibsen's generation the great opponent of man was seen to be society—not just society in its "problem play" aspect, the source of definable, limitable and often remediable misery, but society as a force working through a myriad of obscure agencies and trivial occasions, but working with a power and a mystery comparable to that displayed by the Greek gods or the Elizabethan universe. Or perhaps I should say that Ibsen had the wit to see society in this light; but having seen it, there remained for him the problem of presenting this vision in the theater.

Ibsen's problem as a dramatist was therefore a double one: to present a convincing portrait of a modern individual and still make a hero out of him; and to present a portrait of modern society that is accurate and lifelike but which shows it as operating as an inexorably powerful force upon the tragic hero. And by present, I emphasize that Ibsen had to do all this in terms of the theater. So that although my theme is a general one, it is also a severely limited one. By Ibsen's search for the hero I do not mean merely his search for the *idea* of a hero but his search for the technical means of expressing that vision in the theater. . . .

NORA'S STRUGGLE

I chose *A Doll's House* to show how Ibsen succeeded because it is not generally thought by the public to be a tragedy, and yet Ibsen refers to it in a draft as "The Modern Tragedy.". . . Ibsen suggests, through devices similar to those that we have observed in the earlier plays, a tragic struggle that lies behind the trivial anxieties of a housewife, a struggle involving an heroic figure in conflict with the secret, powerful, and ineluctable forces of society. . . .

The first blow to Nora's happiness falls when the maid

lets in Krogstad. Clearly his visit worries her, although her words tell us little: when Krogstad goes into Helmer's study, Nora goes at once to the stove and stokes the fire—his presence has chilled her.

It is important to grasp this first hint of unpleasant elements in a Doll's House existence because it is closely followed by the first hint of another kind of unpleasantness in the person of Dr. Rank. Within a few seconds of his entrance he has a very important speech.

NORA. Come, Dr. Rank—you want to live yourself.
RANK. To be sure I do. However wretched I may be, I want to drag on as long as possible. All my patients, too, have the same mania. And *it's the same with people whose complaint* is moral. At this very moment Helmer is talking to just such a moral incurable— . . . A fellow named Krogstad, a man you know nothing about—corrupt to the very core of his character. But even he began by announcing, as a matter of vast importance, that he must live!

Now this speech is very important for two reasons: first, because it shows that Rank, like Nora, has a hidden source of disquiet, a physical one—he is wretched in a way that threatens his life; and second, because his speech equates physical illness with moral illness; so that from this point onwards, Ibsen can use physical illness as a symbol of moral illness. . . .

[Krogstad] threatens Nora that if she allows Torvald to dismiss him, he will tell her husband that Nora borrowed from him the money needed to send Torvald away for his health––a terrifying threat in itself because Torvald detests borrowing, but horrifying when Krogstad accuses Nora of forging her dying father's signature to get the money, and threatens her with the legal consequences of forgery.

Nora tries to pretend that the *legal* aspect of the affair leaves her unmoved—if the law does not allow a wife to forge when she wants to spare her father anxiety and to save her husband's life, then the law must be stupid. No, she says, it is impossible—she did it for love.

This is not a very sensible attitude to take, but it represents a desperate attempt to protect her threatened Doll's House existence merely by *asserting* that her home, her family, *must* come first, before legal obligations and suchlike—but Ibsen reinforces this impression of her trying to thrust other considerations aside by using the Christmas tree again. Nora asks the maid to bring in the tree, and place it in the middle of the floor. . . .

But of course mere assertion that her Doll's House values are right, and the values of the outside world are wrong, is useless. Nora soon gets a worse shock; she learns something which terrifies her far more than the threat of mere legal action: her husband, in all innocence, points out that Krogstad's real crime was not forgery, but concealment of forgery. That made him deceitful, and since then he has contaminated his own children with his own moral sickness. . . .

Nora now believes that she is corrupt because of her deceitfulness; she is terrified to think that she may corrupt and poison her own children with a moral corruption as foul as Rank's physical sickness. Rank gives us the size of the horror she faces.

At the curtain of Act I, Nora is still trying to convince herself that this new danger of contaminating her children morally is no more real than the earlier legal threat from Krogstad. "Corrupt *my* children!—Poison *my* home! It's not true! It can never, never be true!"—but her face is "pale with terror"—and she now believes that the poison of moral corruption runs in her veins. She is fighting against Death.

So Nora faces two terrors—the threat of legal action and disgrace, leading to the destruction of her Doll's House; and the certainty of moral disaster for her children if she continues as their mother. The joy has gone out of family life, and Ibsen provides a fitting stage picture for her anguish.

NORA'S HEROISM

Now that Nora is firmly established as in some sense a spiritual incurable, the link between her and Rank, the physical incurable, is immeasurably strengthened. Early in Act II, we hear all about the spinal disease he inherited from his father—and from then on we can see both Rank and Nora as carriers of an obscure and secret poison slowly killing them. . . .

Nora is almost hysterical with terror at the thought of her situation—almost, but it is part of her character that with great heroism she keeps her fears secret to herself; and it is because of her reticence that Rank is dramatically necessary, to symbolize the horror she will not talk about. Nora feels, and we feel, the full awfulness of Rank's illness, and she transfers to herself the same feeling about the moral corruption which she imagines herself to carry. . . .

Nora tries to relieve the superficial part of her anxiety by persuading Torvald to let Krogstad have his job back—that might save her from public disgrace—but she only makes her deeper anxiety worse, because Torvald loses patience and reminds her that her own father was not above suspicion—this increases her sense of being corrupt, because, we recall, she inherited some qualities from her father. And her sense of being infectious, of being a danger to her family as Rank's father proved to him, is increased when Torvald expansively tries to soothe her by saying that of course he would take upon his own shoulders whatever evil threatened her. So her deceit will ruin not only herself by public disgrace, and her children, but her beloved husband. This is the last straw. She now feels a moral leper. Torvald's self-sacrifice would be wonderful, but at the same time, terrible. At all costs it must be prevented—and so begins her somber interview with Dr. Rank, her one last chance of getting enough money to buy off Krogstad's revenge and escape death. . . .

But this interview, although it shows Nora at her best, heroically fighting disaster without whimpering, also shows her at her worst. All this sexual teasing of Rank, for example, with her stockings and her tasteless jokes about his disease—as I read it, Ibsen is showing us here the bad results of her upbringing, first by her father and then by her husband. She can get her own way with men by cajoling, by teasing—and she has learnt no other way more self-respecting. That is why she flirts so cruelly with Rank—not because she gets fun out of it, but because it is the only way she knows of dealing with men. It is the spoilt Nora who does the flirting—it is the heroic woman underneath, the woman of fundamentally sound principles who puts a stop to the nonsense when it begins to offend her sense of rightness. She puts an end to the interview even though it means throwing away her last chance of salvation from a fate that she sees as dreadful.

That is why the scene is important—another instance of heroism.

Nora's doom moves a step nearer: Krogstad calls again, to tell her that instead of informing the police, he intends to blackmail Helmer. This is the end for Nora—when Krogstad leaves, but drops the blackmailing letter into the letter-box, she cries, in genuine anguish, "Torvald, Torvald—now we are lost." Mrs. Linde offers to help by influencing Krogstad and leaves Nora to keep Torvald away from the letter-box until she returns—but so far as Nora is concerned, the end is upon her; as she sees it, the moment has come when the poison must work to its crisis. Like the tarantula's victim, she can only dance a mad dance in a last, vain effort to expel the poison—she expresses her intolerable anxiety in the tarantella. . . .

The last act opens—it is nighttime. Mrs. Linde is waiting for Krogstad to call while the Helmers are upstairs at the fancy-dress party where Nora is to perform her tarantella. Mrs. Linde once loved Krogstad, and proposes marriage to him now. He accepts. A piece of machinery out of a well-made play—the secondary characters are being tidied up, the villain is being reformed in the most economical way. But why bother to reform the villain? For Mrs. Linde after all refuses to let him demand back his blackmailing letter. No, the real point of the scene is to demonstrate the one fundamental truth about women.

I need someone to be a mother to, and your children need a mother. You need me, and I—I need you.

This is Mrs. Linde speaking, the woman who at the beginning of the play had nothing to live for, who had earned her own living, mixed with the outer world, and found life profoundly depressing and aimless without the anchor of a husband and children. This scene describes for us in advance the painful void into which Nora consigns herself at the end of the play. . . .

Ibsen . . . emphasizes the climax of the disease and death theme by bringing on Rank. Nora has danced her tarantella at the party upstairs—her last fling. At the same party, Rank had enjoyed his last fling—at the champagne—before retiring to his death-bed. The last link which Ibsen forges between the two victims of poison and corruption is that their deathwarrants share the same letter-box: Rank leaves behind him a visiting-card marked with a black cross, a sign that he has crawled away to die; the card lies beside Krogstad's letter to Torvald, and when Torvald reads that, Nora must die so as not to inflict her moral disease on others; physical and moral corruption are to burn themselves out together.

She waits for the right moment, when Torvald promises again to shoulder his wife's burdens. He, of course, is merely romanticizing; she takes him seriously, and sends him off to read the fatal letter. She will go out and drown herself to prevent this heroic sacrifice.

Ibsen's Modern Hero

Helmer does not perform a miracle when he reads Krogstad's blackmailing letter. He explodes into vulgar rage—he calls his wife a hypocrite, a liar, a criminal; he throws her father into her face: "I ought to have foreseen it. All your father's want of principle—all your father's want of principle you have inherited—no religion, no morality, no sense of duty!" This is an aspect of the problem which had not occurred to Nora before—but she remains quiet—perhaps she is a victim like Rank, as well as a carrier of corruption.

The miracle has not happened. Nora realizes that she has been living an illusion; and one does not die for illusions if one recognizes them for such. It is irrelevant to her that a note should arrive from Krogstad returning her I.O.U.'s, that Helmer should say, with sickening egotism, "I am saved! Nora, I am saved." That part of her problem, the legal or public side, now assumes its rightful place as trivial compared with the moral problem, which remains. Nora realizes numbly that her life has been an elaborate make-believe. She does not say so just yet—she is cold, almost silent. But her costume speaks for her. As she discards her illusions, so she discards her fancy-dress and her black cloak and shawl, and appears in her everyday dress—to symbolize her entry into a world of cold fact and commonsense.

From her new, sad viewpoint, her notion of heredity becomes as wide as ours, the audience's, has long become. She agrees that she is not fit, in her present state of moral health, to have charge of the education of her children. But Helmer's words have made her bitterly aware that the poison did not originate with her:

> I have had great injustice done me, Torvald, first by father, and then by you.

They have both treated her as a doll-child. It is the men who run society who have condemned Nora to a stultifying life. That is the real crime, the real corruption, as she clearly sees, not her forgery or her little lies, but the male conspiracy to debase the female; and she now recognizes that she had begun to bring up her own children as if they too were dolls. It is the Doll's House attitude that is the corruption which must not be transmitted. She must go into a hostile world and educate herself. . . .

What has Ibsen done in this play that he did not do before? He has, above all, exercised the art of concentration. He has written a modern play about a modern woman in a modern situation, but he adds new stature and a new dimension to it by concentrating different kinds of imagery to suggest that society works upon Nora like some dreadful, hidden, and inexorable disease. The final draft version of the play lacks this concentration, and this power. He guides our attention to this theme through his verbal imagery (e.g., Rank's first speech), but he maintains it by a concentration of suggestive detail—Nora's black shawl, the sympathetic night light of Act III, the figure of Rank, the tarantella-dance—all of these help to create the sense of fatality; and Nora's consistent fight against that, a fight in which she will sacrifice no basic principles however desperate her situation, makes her into a heroine. Ibsen has discovered his modern hero.

I suggest that it was some such vision that Ibsen had in mind when he called the play "The Modern Tragedy." I suggest that you will find themes of similar or greater majesty created in later plays, which must be seen not as realistic plays, or, in contradiction, as plays full of verbal symbolism, but as plays filled with metaphors and images drawn from the whole range of theatrical material; plays filled thereby with a sense of the poetry of life, even of modern life. My point may be summarized if I say that Ibsen's prose plays present the poetry of life in the imagery of the theater.

Ibsen Is a Radical Moralist and Romantic Rebel

Leif Longum

Professor of Norwegian Literature at the University of
Bergen and author of numerous studies on Norwegian
playwrights and literature, Leif Longum writes that Ibsen's work is representative of Norwegian literature and
cultural heritage. While Ibsen believed in the role of the
writer to "serve the cause of national identity and independence," he remained an independent rebel, never
embracing the various groups that approached him for
their causes. His plays were not simply political mes-
sages; rather, he "encourages a re-examination of the
truths of today—which become the lies of tomorrow."

. . . "Henrik Ibsen lives among us even today," Helge Krog
wrote in 1928; "fragments of his intellectual universe [have]
entered into our consciousness. . . ."

What Helge Krog here notes is how Ibsen's presence in Norwegian life and literature for more than a hundred years has
influenced our way of thinking and become part of our cultural heritage. This kind of influence is even more difficult to
define and measure than a purely literary one. At the center is
a vision of the free, unique individual, striving to achieve self-
realization in despite of the forces of an oppressive society. One
can argue that this extreme individualism belongs to the nineteenth century and that its glorification of the lonely individual
pitted against society leads to isolation and sterility (as Helge
Krog showed in his play about "the crisis of individualism,"
Breakup, 1936). The fact is that it still permeates our habits of
thought and that the vitality and moral force of Ibsen's work
have helped to keep it alive.

Excerpted from Leif Longum, "In the Shadow of Ibsen: His Influence on Norwegian
Drama and on Literary Attitudes," in *Review of National Literatures*, vol. 12, *Norway*,
1983. Reprinted by permission of Griffon House Press, Inc. Notes in the original have
been omitted in this reprint.

Ibsen himself had a strong belief in his own mission and again and again stressed the moral obligation of the writer. "It is not for a comfortable livelihood that I struggle," he wrote in a letter to the Swedish-Norwegian king in 1866, asking for financial support,

> but for the calling which I unwaveringly believe and know that God has placed upon me—the calling which, to me, seems the most important and most necessary in Norway, namely, to awaken the people and make it think great thoughts.

Later Ibsen became more pessimistic about his own countrymen and about his own ability to act as his nation's conscience. But even in his last, self-tormenting plays he remained a moralist.

Ibsen was not alone among the writers of his time to stress the writer's high calling. In this respect he typifies a Romantic tradition, defined in Shelley's famous declaration from 1821: "Poets are the unacknowledged legislators of the world." This view of the writer was shared by Ibsen and his contemporaries, writers and audience alike. It has survived until today, perhaps more persistently in Norway than in most other countries. Part of the explanation is that the golden age of Norwegian literature in the latter part of the nineteenth century was also a time of national awakening. When the four-hundred-year-old union with Denmark was dissolved in 1814 and supplanted by a looser union with Sweden, Norwegian writers were called upon to serve the cause of national identity and independence. (The situation of the writer in the new African states today presents striking parallels.) From Henrik Wergeland onward, a majority of writers accepted the challenge, engaging themselves in the cultural and political struggle and creating what the historian Ernst Sars called a "poetocracy" in Norway. The undisputed figurehead of this radical poetocracy was Ibsen's friend and contemporary Bjørnstjerne Bjørnson. Ibsen remained more aloof from day-to-day politics.

IBSEN IS AN INDEPENDENT REBEL

As his world reputation grew, different groups tried to enlist him on their side in the ideological battle. Ibsen vehemently protested against being drawn into these battles. He was not fighting for temporary reforms but dreamt of the "revolt of the human spirit." He wanted, as he wrote in a letter of 1882, "to be like a solitary sniper at the outposts and to operate on his own." He attacked the established society, rejected the whole concept of the State (like the anarchists), expressed his belief in the future of oppressed groups like women and the workers; but he was also full of contempt for the progressive politicians of the day. Not surprisingly he was, on different occasions, attacked both by the Left and the Right.

Nevertheless, I think it is correct to say that, both in his lifetime and afterwards, Ibsen has been seen in Norway as primarily a *radical* writer (definitely not as a conservative, as Arnold Hauser maintains in *The Social History of Art*). As such he stands out as one of the dominant figures in the unbroken tradition of literary radicalism in Norway, stretching from Wergeland to the young Marxist-Leninist writers of today.

In an article from 1932 Helge Krog sees Ibsen as the representative example of the writer as rebel. Krog takes as his starting point the celebration of the Ibsen centennial in 1928. It lasted an entire week and was, for Helge Krog, a trying experience. "But what really did me in were the *speeches*," Krog writes. The speakers had come from all over the world and represented all kinds of value systems and ideologies. But every one of them had nothing but praise for Ibsen. Was this because all of Ibsen's visions and hopes for mankind had now been fulfilled, Krog asks. Of course not. The speakers themselves disproved it: they represented all the characters Ibsen had unmasked in his plays—the pillars of society, the hypocrites, the self-deceivers. Now they were trying to disarm the rebel with their praise, to make him into a harmless classic. But so far they have not succeeded, Helge Krog concludes.

Yet, to present Ibsen as a radical writer, as Krog and many before and after him have done, is not without its problems. For one thing, Ibsen's position seems to have changed during his long career. Furthermore, only a limited number of his plays can be called social or political, such as *Pillars of Society*, *A Doll's House*, *Ghosts*, and *An Enemy of the People*, and even these plays cannot be reduced to a simple political message....

What all this adds up to is that even as simple a play as *An Enemy of the People* contains a basic ambiguity, an ambiguity that is one of the striking features of all of Ibsen's work. Robert Brustein demonstrates this convincingly in *The Theatre of Revolt* (Boston, 1964), a study of eight playwrights from Ibsen to Genet. As Brustein sees him, Ibsen is the first in a line of Romantic rebels:

> Discontented with everything but a new beginning, Ibsen finds
> it impossible to identify with any existing parties, systems, or

programs, or even to ally himself with any existing revolutionary principles. His revolt, in short, is so individualistic that it transcends politics entirely.

Ibsen, Brustein says, "is hostile to all movements based on a social concept of man." His purpose is "not superficial changes in the social structure but a complete alteration in the moral nature of man." It is worth stressing that Brustein does not make Ibsen into an *apolitical* writer. He only shows how impossible it is to fit him into any conventional political category.

IBSEN'S PLAYS ARE TIMELESS

Others—both in Ibsen's own time and later, in Norway and abroad—have rejected all attempts to make Ibsen a radical. Ibsen's plays, they argue, have a timeless quality that places them far above the conflicts of his society. In Norwegian Ibsen criticism this view was greatly stimulated after the last war by impulses from Anglo-American New Criticism. A representative example is *Henrik Ibsens realisme* (Oslo, 1957) by Daniel Haakonsen. Haakonsen's main point is that Ibsen in his realistic plays is only superficially concerned with temporary problems. Beneath the surface realism he presents a timeless conflict: man confronting the eternal forces of existence.

Haakonsen undeniably has a point. The fact that Ibsen's realistic plays have appealed to audiences and readers at different times and in different cultures, shows that his conflicts transcend their historical setting. But in the literary climate of Norway today—strongly influenced by the political awakening and radicalization that followed the student revolt of 1968—the ahistorical understanding advocated by the New Criticism is questioned. Its basic understanding of the nature of a literary work, and its method of analysing a literary text, is no longer accepted as neutral or non-political. Its stress on the timeless quality of literature in reality serves an ideological function. It is a way of blunting the critical potential of great writing, like Ibsen's. A single example may serve as illustration. In a school edition of *A Doll's House* published in 1969, the Norwegian Ibsen scholar Else Høst . . . writes in a commentary that "in our days the feminist debate in its original form has long ago disappeared; at any rate, its ideas do not belong to those that most strongly engage the minds of the present generation." In the 1950s such a statement would have been widely accepted. Today critical attention is again directed towards the historical and sociocritical aspects of Ibsen's plays, exactly those aspects that Else Høst . . . found of little or no relevance for our time. . . .

For a long time Ibsen has been acknowledged as the great master of modern drama (although his plays no longer serve as formal models for new ambitious playwrights). With regard to his general influence, moral more than esthetic, it is felt as a continued challenge. Part of the secret of this challenge is the ambiguity or unresolved tension of Ibsen's plays. His extreme individualism is a legacy from nineteenth-century liberalism, and still a part of our habits of thought—for some a negative influence to be thrown off, for others a living inspiration. Both positions can be defended with reference to Ibsen's plays. That is to say: Ibsen's untiring questioning of all values and beliefs, including his own, makes it impossible to pin him down once and for all. Instead, he encourages a re-examination of the truths of today—which become the lies of tomorrow.

CHRONOLOGY

1828

Henrik Ibsen is born on March 20 in Skien, Norway, to Knud and Marichen Ibsen.

1835

Financial difficulties force the Ibsens to move to Venstøp.

1844

The Ibsens move back to Skien, and Henrik moves to Grimstad to become an apothecary's apprentice; he lives here for six years.

1846

A housemaid gives birth to Henrik's illegitimate son, Hans Jacob Henriksen; Ibsen assumes partial support of the child for fourteen years.

1849

Ibsen writes his first play, *Catiline*, but it is rejected by the Christiania Theatre.

1850

Catiline is published privately under the pseudonym of Brynjolf Bjarme; in April, Ibsen prepares for university entrance exams, but he does not pass them; he finishes his second play, *Warrior's Barrow*, which is performed later in the year at the Christiania Theatre.

1851

Ibsen moves to Bergen for an appointment as a theater assistant (dramatic author) in Ole Bull's Norwegian theater; during this time he publishes articles and poems in various periodicals.

1852

Ibsen tours theaters in Dresden, Copenhagen, and Hamburg to study stage direction.

1853–1855

Ibsen's plays *St. John's Night, Warrior's Barrow,* and *Lady In-ger* are performed in Bergen with little success.

1856

The Feast at Solhaug is performed in Bergen; Ibsen meets fu-ture wife, Suzannah Thoresen.

1857

Olaf Liljekrans is performed in Bergen; Ibsen accepts a post at the Norwegian Theatre in Møllergaten.

1858

At age thirty, Ibsen marries Suzannah Thoresen; *The Vikings at Helgeland* is first rejected in Copenhagen for being too crude, but it is later produced at the Norwegian Theatre, by Ibsen.

1859

Henrik and Suzannah's son, Sigurd, is born on December 23.

1862

Ibsen is awarded a grant to travel extensively to collect Nor-wegian folktales; the Norwegian Theatre goes bankrupt and Ibsen loses his job; *Love's Comedy* is printed in a journal.

1863

Deeply in debt, Ibsen is appointed literary consultant to the reestablished Christiania Theatre; he is later awarded a travel grant to study in Rome.

1864

The Pretenders is directed by Ibsen and performed in Chris-tiania; Ibsen travels to Copenhagen, Berlin, Vienna, Tri-este,Venice, Genzano, and Rome, where his family finally joins him.

1866

Brand is published in Copenhagen and well received in Scandinavia; Ibsen receives a lifetime annual government grant for his writing; his financial situation improves.

1867

Peer Gynt is published in Copenhagen.

1868

After traveling for a few weeks, Ibsen takes up permanent residence with his family in Dresden.

1869

Ibsen is decorated by King Carl XV as a knight with the Vasa order; he travels to Egypt as Norway's representative at the opening of the Suez Canal; *The League of Youth* is published.

1871

Ibsen in honored by Denmark with the Order of Dannebrog; his selected poems are published.

1872

Edmund Gosse is the first to write critical works on Ibsen in England; his articles on Ibsen are published in various journals over the next couple of years.

1873

Ibsen is decorated by Norway with the Knight's Order of St. Olaf; *The Emperor and the Galilean* is published.

1874

Ibsen is honored by Christiania students in a torchlight procession.

1875

Ibsen moves from Dresden to Munich, where he will remain for the next three years.

1876

Catherine Ray is the first to translate a complete work of Ibsen's (*The Emperor and the Galilean*) into English.

1877

Ibsen receives an honorary doctorate from the University of Uppsala, Sweden; *Pillars of Society* is published.

1879

A Doll's House is published.

1880

Ibsen moves to Rome for the winter, where he remains for the next five years; an adaptation of *Pillars of Society* is performed in London, the first Ibsen play on an English stage.

1881

Ghosts is published.

1882

The Child Wife, an adaptation of *A Doll's House,* is performed in Milwaukee, the first presentation of Ibsen in the United States. *An Enemy of the People* is also published this year.

1884

The Wild Duck is published.

1885

Ibsen travels extensively through Norway, then returns to Munich for the next six years.

1886

Rosmersholm is published.

1888

The Lady from the Sea is published.

1889

A Doll's House is performed in London; it is the first non-adapted production of Ibsen in England.

1890

William Archer publishes the first collected edition of Ibsen's plays in English; *Hedda Gabler* is published.

1892

The Master Builder is published.

1894

Little Eyolf is published.

1896

John Gabriel Borkman is published.

1898

Ibsen receives many honors on his seventieth birthday; festivities take place in Christiania, Copenhagen, and Stockholm in the spring; publication of his collected works in Norwegian and German begins.

1899

When We Dead Awaken is published.

1900

Ibsen suffers a stroke and is unable to continue writing.

1906

Ibsen dies on May 23.

FOR FURTHER RESEARCH

BIOGRAPHIES

Edvard Beyer, trans. by Marie Wells, *Ibsen: The Man and His Work*. London: Souvenir Press, 1978.

George B. Bryan, *An Ibsen Companion: A Dictionary-Guide to Life, Works, and Critical Reception of Henrik Ibsen*. Westport, CT: Greenwood, 1984.

Robert Ferguson, *Henrik Ibsen: A New Biography*. London: Richard Cohen Books, 1996.

Hans Heiberg, *Ibsen: A Portrait of the Artist*. Coral Gables, FL: University of Miami Press, 1969.

Halvdan Koht, *Life of Ibsen*. Trans. Einar Haugen and A.E. Santaniello. New York: Benjamin Bloom, 1971.

Henry Rose, *Henrik Ibsen: Poet, Mystic, and Moralist*. Brooklyn: Haskell House, 1972.

CRITICISM

Asbjørn Aarseth, *The Torpedo and the Greenhouse: Two Perspectives on Henrik Ibsen*. Minneapolis: University of Minnesota, 1990.

Gretchen P. Ackerman, *Ibsen and the English Stage, 1889–1903*. New York: Garland, 1987.

Clela Allphin-Hoggatt, *Women in the Plays of Henrik Ibsen*. New York: Revisionist Press, 1975.

William Archer, *William Archer on Ibsen: The Major Essays, 1889–1919*. Contributions in Drama and Theatre Studies, No. 13. Westport, CT: Greenwood, 1984.

Harold Clurman, *Ibsen*. New York: Macmillan, 1977.

Errol Durbach, A Doll's House: *Ibsen's Myth of Transformation*. Boston: Twayne, 1991.

Errol Durbach, ed., *Ibsen and the Theatre: Essays in Celebration of the 150th Anniversary of Henrik Ibsen's Birth*. London: Macmillan, 1980.

Rolf Fjelde, *Ibsen: A Collection of Critical Essays*. Englewood Cliffs, NJ: Prentice Hall, 1965.

Ronald Gray, *Ibsen: A Dissenting View*. London: Cambridge University Press, 1977.

Naomi Lebowitz, *Ibsen and the Great World*. Baton Rouge:

Louisiana State University Press, 1990.

Charles R. Lyons, ed., *Critical Essays on Henrik Ibsen.* Boston: G.K. Hall, 1987.

Frederick J. Marker, *Ibsen's Lively Art: A Performance Study of the Major Plays.* Cambridge: Cambridge University Press, 1989.

James McFarlane, *Ibsen and Meaning: Studies, Essays and Prefaces, 1953–87.* Chester Springs, PA: Dufour Editions, 1989.

James McFarlane, ed., *The Cambridge Companion to Ibsen.* Cambridge: Cambridge University Press, 1994.

Michael Leverson Meyer, *Ibsen on File.* London: Methuen, 1985.

John Northam, *Ibsen: A Critical Study.* Cambridge: Cambridge University Press, 1973.

Robert A. Schanke, *Ibsen in America: A Century of Change.* Metuchen, NJ: Scarecrow Press, 1988.

Kirsten Shepherd-Barr, *Ibsen and Early Modernist Theatre, 1890–1900.* Contributions in Drama and Theatre Studies, No. 78. Westport, CT: Greenwood, 1997.

Joan Templeton, *Ibsen's Women.* Port Chester, NY: Cambridge University Press, 1997.

Theoharis Constantine Theoharis, *Ibsen's Drama: Right Action and Tragic Joy.* New York: St. Martin's Press, 1996.

NOTES AND LETTERS

Henrik Ibsen, *Correspondence of Henrik Ibsen.* Ed., Mary Morison. Brooklyn: Haskell House, 1970.

Henrik Ibsen, *From Ibsen's Workshop: Notes, Scenarios, and Drafts of the Modern Plays.* Trans. A.G. Chater. New York: Da Capo Press, 1978.

Henrik Ibsen, *Speeches and New Letters.* Trans. Arne Kildal. Brooklyn: Haskell House, 1972.

HISTORICAL OR LITERARY INTEREST

Richard Foulkes, *Church and Stage in Victorian England.* Port Chester, NY: Cambridge University Press, 1997.

Janet Garton, ed., *Contemporary Norwegian Women's Writing.* Chester Springs, PA: Dufour Editions, 1996.

Anthony Jenkins, *The Making of Victorian Drama.* Port Chester, NY: Cambridge University Press, 1991.

Theodore Jorgenson, *Norwegian Literature in Medieval and Early Modern Times.* Westport, CT: Greenwood, 1978.

Penny Kane, *Victorian Families in Fact and Fiction.* New York: St. Martin's Press, 1995.

Orm Overland, *The Western Home: A Literary History of Norwegian America.* Champaign: University of Illinois Press, 1997.

WORKS BY HENRIK IBSEN

Catiline, 1850

Warrior's Barrow, 1850

Norma, 1851

St. John's Night, 1853

Lady Inger, 1855

The Feast at Solhaug, 1856

Olaf Liljekrans, 1857

The Vikings at Helgeland,
1858

Love's Comedy, 1862

The Pretenders, 1863

Brand, 1866

Peer Gynt, 1867

The League of Youth, 1869

Poems, 1871

*The Emperor and the
Galilean,* 1873

Pillars of Society, 1877

A Doll's House, 1879

Ghosts, 1881

An Enemy of the People,
1882

The Wild Duck, 1884

Rosmersholm, 1886

The Lady from the Sea, 1888

Hedda Gabler, 1890

The Master Builder, 1892

Little Eyolf, 1894

John Gabriel Borkman, 1896

When We Dead Awaken,
1899

Index

women
    freedom of, 100–101, 108
    Ibsen's sympathy/empathy for,
        25, 97–98, 100–101, 114–18
    male attitudes toward, 116–17
    in marriage, 98–99
    portrayed through Ibsen, 37, 38,
        39, 103–104, 107–108, 141
    stereotype of, 112
    writing plays, 131
Women's Rights League of
    Norway, 97

Yeats, W.B., 57